PHOTOSHOP 6

in easy steps

ROBERT SHUFFLEBOTHAM

**COMPUTER
STEP**

In easy steps is an imprint of Computer Step
Southfield Road . Southam
Warwickshire CV47 OFB . England

http://www.ineasysteps.com

Notice of Liability
Every effort has been made to ensure that this book contains accurate and current information. However, Computer Step and the author shall not be liable for any loss or damage suffered by readers as a result of any information contained herein.

Trademarks
Photoshop® is a registered trademark of Adobe Systems Incorporated. All other trademarks are acknowledged as belonging to their respective companies.

Printed and bound in the United Kingdom

ISBN 1-84078-123-8

Table Of Contents

Basic Theory

An understanding of the basics of colour is important if you are to get the best out of Photoshop. Refer back to this section from time to time. As your understanding of Photoshop grows, so will your appreciation of the concepts of colour that underpin the whole process of image capture and image manipulation.

This section also covers RGB, CMYK and monitor calibration.

Covers

Chapter One

Bitmaps and Vectors

Photoshop is an image-editing application with a wealth of tools and commands for working on digital images or bitmaps. There are utilities for retouching, colour correcting, compositing and more. There are also over 90 functional and creative filters that can be applied to entire images, or selected areas within images.

A bitmap image consists of a rectangular grid, or raster, of pixels – in concept, very much like a mosaic. When you edit a bitmap you are editing the colour values of individual pixels or groups of pixels.

Image-editing applications differ fundamentally from vector-based applications such as Adobe Illustrator and Macromedia FreeHand. In these applications, you work with objects that can be moved, scaled, transformed, stacked and deleted as individual or grouped objects, but all the time each exists as a complete, separate object.

These applications are called vector drawing packages, as each object is defined by a mathematical formula. Because of this, they are resolution-independent – you can scale vector drawings up or down (either in the originating application or in a page layout application such as QuarkXPress or Adobe PageMaker) and they will still print smoothly and crisply.

You should always try to scan an image at, or slightly larger than, the size at which you intend to use it. This means you will avoid having to increase the size of the image.

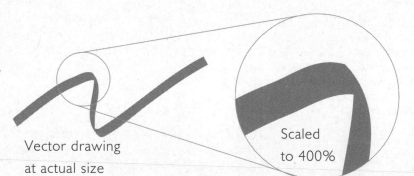

Vector drawing at actual size

Scaled to 400%

In contrast, bitmaps are created at a set resolution – a fixed number of pixels per inch. If you scan an image at a specific resolution, then double its size, you are effectively halving its resolution (unless you add more pixels). You are likely to end up with a blocky, jagged image, as you have increased the size of the individual pixels that make up the bitmap image.

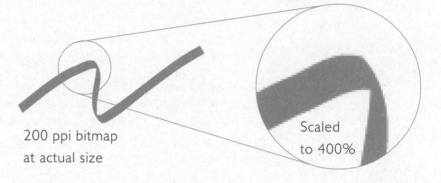

200 ppi bitmap
at actual size

Scaled
to 400%

Bitmaps and Bit-depth

An important factor when the digital data for an image is captured, typically at the scanning stage, is its bit-depth. Bit-depth refers to the amount of digital storage space used to record information about the colour of a pixel. The more bits you use, the more colour information you can store to describe the colour of a pixel – but also, the larger the file size you end up with.

More, rather than less, colour information is usually desirable, as this means the image can represent more shades of colour, with finer transitions between colours and greater density of colour, leading to a more realistic image.

To output realistic images using PostScript technology an image should be able to represent 256 grey levels. A 24-bit scan is sufficient for recording 256 grey levels for each of the Red, Green and Blue channels, resulting in a possible combination of over 16 million colours.

Ideally, when you work on images in Photoshop you will do so using a 24-bit monitor capable of displaying over 16 million colours. This ensures that you see all the colour detail in the image. Although you can work on images using only thousands of colours, for best results, especially where colour reproduction is important, you need to work with as many colours as possible.

Pixels and Resolution

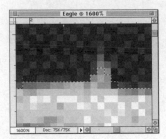

Pixels

A pixel is the smallest element in a bitmap image such as a scan. Pixel is short for 'picture element'. Zoom in on an image in Photoshop and you will start to see the individual pixels – the fundamental building blocks – that make up the image. When working in Photoshop, you are editing pixels, changing their colour, shade and brightness.

Resolution

A key factor when working on bitmap images is resolution. This is measured in pixels per inch (ppi).

Pixels can vary in size. If you have an image with a resolution of 100 ppi, each pixel would be 1/100th of an inch square. In an image with a resolution of 300 ppi, each pixel would be 1/300th of an inch square – giving a much finer, less blocky result.

Printer resolution measured in dots per inch (dpi) is not the same as image resolution measured in pixels per inch (ppi). Printer dots are a fixed size, pixels can vary in size.

When working on images that will eventually be printed on a printing press, you need to work on high-resolution images. These are scanned images whose resolution is twice the halftone screen frequency (measured in lines per inch – lpi) that will be used for final output – that is when you output to bromide or film.

For example, for a final output screen frequency of 150 lpi – a typical screen frequency used for glossy magazines – you need to scan your image at a resolution of 300 ppi.

Resolutions of double the screen frequency are important for images with fine lines, repeating patterns or textures. You can achieve acceptable results, especially when printing at screen frequencies greater than 133 lpi, using resolutions of 1½ times the final screen frequency.

Images intended for multimedia presentations or the World Wide Web need only be 72 ppi, which is effectively the screen resolution.

To work with images for positional purposes only, as long as you can get accurate enough on-screen results and laser proofs, you can work with much lower resolutions.

RGB and CMYK Colour Models

As you start working with Adobe Photoshop there are two colour models that you need to be aware of. These are the RGB (Red, Green, Blue) and CMYK (Cyan, Magenta, Yellow and BlacK) colour models.

RGB is important because it mirrors the way the human eye perceives colour. It is the model used by scanners and digital cameras to capture colour information in digital format, and it is the way that your computer monitor describes colour.

Red, green and blue are referred to as the 'additive primaries'. You can add varying proportions of the three colours to produce millions of different colours – but still a more limited range (or 'gamut') than in nature, due to the limitations of the phosphor screen coating of the monitor. If you add 100% red, green and blue light together, you get white. You produce the 'secondary' colours when you add red and blue to get magenta; green and blue to get cyan; red and green to get yellow.

The CMYK colour model is referred to as the 'subtractive' colour model. It is important because this is the colour model used by printing presses.

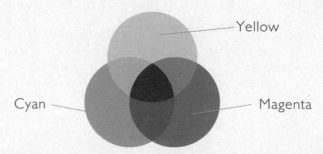

If you subtract all cyan, magenta and yellow when printing you end up with the complete absence of colour – white.

On the printing press, cyan, magenta, yellow and black are combined to simulate a huge variety of colours. Printers add black because, although in theory, if you combine 100% each of cyan, magenta and yellow you produce black, in reality, because of impurities in the dyes, you only get a muddy brown.

Colour Gamuts

Colour gamut refers to the range of colours that a specific device is capable of producing. There are millions of colours in the visible spectrum that the eye can discern. Scanners, monitors and printing presses cannot reproduce every colour in the visible spectrum – the range of colours they are capable of producing is their gamut.

From the desktop publishing point of view, the process of capturing digital colour information, viewing and manipulating this on-screen and then finally printing the image using coloured inks is complicated, because the gamut of a colour monitor is different to the gamut of CMYK and PANTONE inks.

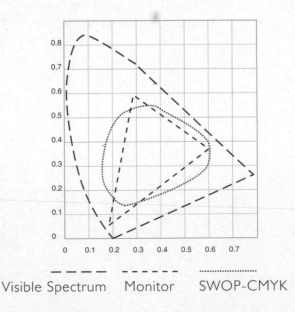

Visible Spectrum   Monitor   SWOP-CMYK

There are colours (especially vibrant yellows and deep blues) that can be displayed on a monitor but cannot be printed using traditional CMYK inks.

Typically, when you work in Photoshop, you will work in RGB (Red, Green, Blue) mode. RGB mode is faster to work in than CMYK mode, and in RGB mode all Photoshop options and commands are available to you. When you have finished making necessary adjustments and corrections to the image, you will need to convert it to CMYK mode, before saving/exporting the image in EPS or TIFF format for use in a page layout application such as Adobe PageMaker or QuarkXPress.

When you convert from RGB to CMYK mode, Photoshop converts out-of-gamut colours (in this case, colours that can be seen on screen, but not printed) into their nearest printable equivalent.

Colour Management

No two devices that represent colour, from scanner to monitor to printer, will reproduce colour in exactly the same way. The aim of a colour management system is to ensure, as far as possible, that the colours you see on your screen will be as close as possible to the colours you see in the finished work, whether in print or on screen.

Colour management settings are available so that you can choose a colour management workflow most suitable to your needs.

Using the Colour Settings dialogue box you can define how you manage colour in your images as you work in Photoshop.

 The very first time you launch Photoshop 6 you will be prompted to choose your colour management settings.

1 To specify colour management settings for your Photoshop working environment, launch Photoshop, then choose Edit > Colour Settings (Command/Ctrl+Shift+K).

2 Choose the most appropriate setting for your intended final output from the Settings pop-up list. For example, if you are using Photoshop for images that will be used in multimedia presentations, or on the World Wide Web, choose Web Graphic Defaults. If you are working with images that will be colour separated then printed using CMYK inks, choose Europe or US Prepress Defaults as appropriate.

Custom
Other
Color Management Off
ColorSync Workflow
Emulate Photoshop 4
✓ Europe Prepress Defaults
Japan Prepress Defaults
Photoshop 5 Default Spaces
U.S. Prepress Defaults
Web Graphics Defaults

3 Leave Advanced Mode option deselected unless you need to change one of the advanced settings.

4 Only make changes to the default settings when you have gained experience of using Photoshop and you have reason for making changes, or if you have consulted with your commercial printer and they have suggested changes to suit your specific output requirements.

If you feel that you are not achieving good colour in printed output, consult your commercial printer about creating custom settings for colour management.

A CMS (Colour Management System) is used to translate colours accurately from one colour device to another. It attempts to represent a colour consistently from the colour space in which the image was created to the colour space used at output, making adjustments so that colour is displayed as consistently as possible across a range of monitors and other devices.

Color Settings

Settings: Europe Prepress Defaults ▼

☐ Advanced Mode

Working Spaces
RGB: Adobe RGB (1998) ▼
CMYK: Euroscale Coated v2 ▼
Gray: Dot Gain 15% ▼
Spot: Dot Gain 15% ▼

Color Management Policies
RGB: Preserve Embedded Profiles ▼
CMYK: Preserve Embedded Profiles ▼
Gray: Preserve Embedded Profiles ▼
Profile Mismatches: ☒ Ask When Opening ☒ Ask When Pasting
Missing Profiles: ☒ Ask When Opening

Description
Europe Prepress Defaults: Preparation of content for common press conditions in Europe.

OK
Cancel
Load...
Save...
☒ Preview

---

5 To get a better understanding of how the settings work in the Colour Settings dialogue box, roll you cursor over the pop-up lists. The Description area at the bottom of the palette updates with information on how the options affects the image.

Monitor Calibration

It is important to calibrate your monitor so that colours in your image are displayed accurately. Calibrating your monitor should eliminate any colour casts (typically reddish or blueish) on your monitor and ensure that the monitor displays greys as neutrally as possible.

Use the Adobe Gamma utility to calibrate the monitor you are using and to define the RGB colour space that your monitor can display.

Once you have calibrated your monitor, Photoshop can compensate for the differences between the colour space in which your image resides and the colour space of the monitor you are using.

The Adobe Gamma utility enables you to calibrate the contrast and brightness, gamma (midtones), colour balance and the white point of the monitor. Calibration settings that you create are saved as an ICC (International Colour Consortium) profile with a .icm extension.

Use the Adobe Gamma Wizard if you are do not have previous experience of calibrating a monitor.

For monitor calibration to be effective, you should not adjust the brightness and contrast settings on your monitor after you have completed the calibration process, and you must ensure that the lighting conditions within the room remain constant.

Hardware-based colour calibration utilities are more accurate than the Adobe Gamma utility. You should use only one calibration utility. Colours may appear incorrectly if you use more than one utility.

| (Windows) Choose Settings > Control Panel from the Start Menu. Double-click the Adobe Gamma icon to display the dialog.
(Macintosh) Use the Apple menu to choose Control Panel > Adobe Gamma.

2 Choose Step by Step Wizard, then click the Next button.

Leave your monitor turned on for at least 30 minutes before you calibrate. This allows the phosphors time to warm up fully and for the display to stabilise.

3 Click the Load button to choose a monitor profile which matches the monitor you are using most closely. (Windows) Profiles are stored in the Windows\ System\ Colour folder. (Mac) Profiles

are stored in the System\ColorSync Profiles folder. Profiles should be available from your monitor manufacturer's Web site, or you can try: www.microsoft.com/hwtest/hcl/. Click the Next button.

4 Adjust the Brightness and Contrast settings of your monitor. Refer to the monitor handbook if you are unsure of how to adjust these settings. Click the Next button.

5 Only change the Phosphors pop-up if you know that your monitor's phosphors are different from the default selection. Click the Next button.

6 With the View Single Gamma Only option selected, drag the
Gamma slider until the square in the middle of the patterned
lines fades, as far as possible,
into the pattern. This defines
the brightness of the midtones
on your monitor. (Un-focus
your eyes slightly to help
achieve the correct result.)
Click the Next button.

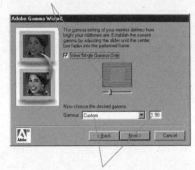

7 For Desired Gamma choose a target gamma. This option is
not available on Windows systems which cannot control the
monitor. If you intend to prepare images for the World
Wide Web or multimedia presentations, choose a gamma of
2.2. If you intend to print images using CMYK inks, you
typically choose a gamma of 1.8. Click Next.

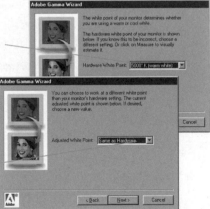

8 Leave the Hardware White
Point on the default setting
unless you know this to be
inaccurate. Click Next.

9 Leave Adjusted White
Point on Same as
Hardware unless you want
to view the image at a
different colour temperature to that set by the monitor's
factory specified setting. Click Next.

10 Click the Finish button to save settings as an .icm
compatible profile. Name the profile and save it to the
ColorSync Profiles folder.

The Working Environment

This section covers the basics of the Photoshop working environment, getting you used to the Photoshop window, the Toolbox, palettes and a number of standard Photoshop conventions that you will find useful as you develop your Photoshop skills.

It also covers the basics of printing composite images to a colour inkjet printer as well as techniques for undoing commands as you work on your images.

Covers

Chapter Two

The Photoshop Screen Environment

There are three 'screen modes' to choose from when working on images in Photoshop. The screen mode icons are located at the bottom of the toolbox. Full screen with menu bar mode is useful when working on individual images because it clears away the clutter of the Finder environment (Mac) or the Windows desktop. Use Full screen mode to see the image without the distraction of other screen elements, and without any other colours interfering with the colours in your image.

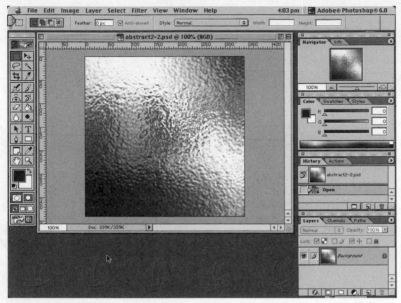

Standard screen mode

Full screen
with menu bar
mode

Full screen mode

| | Click this icon to return to Standard screen mode.

2 Click this icon to go to Full screen with menu bar mode.

3 Click this icon to go to Full screen mode. Press the Tab key to hide/show the Toolbox and palettes.

4 Click the Jump To button to launch ImageReady. (See page 200).

Command (often referred to as 'Apple' on the Mac) and Ctrl (Windows), and Alt (Mac) and Alt (Windows) are used identically as modifier keys. Shift is standard on both platforms.

Windows Environment

The Windows environment offers identical functionality to the Macintosh environment, as you can see from a comparison of the Windows and Macintosh screen shots.

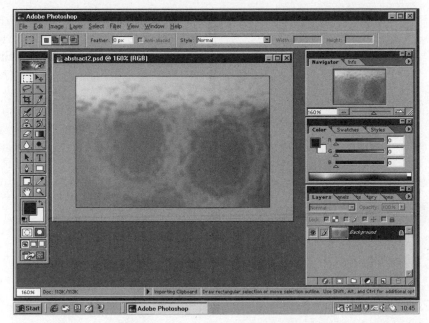

Windows users can use the right mouse button to access context sensitive menus; Mac users can hold down the Ctrl key and press their single mouse button.

The Image Window

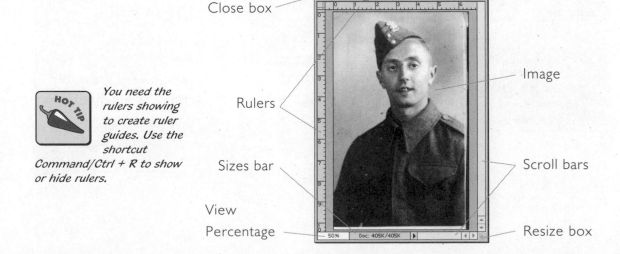

Title bar

Close box

Image

Rulers

Scroll bars

You need the rulers showing to create ruler guides. Use the shortcut Command/Ctrl + R to show or hide rulers.

Sizes bar

View

Percentage

Resize box

Using the Toolbox

There are a number of useful general techniques that relate to choosing tools in the Toolbox, including those from the expanded range of hidden tool pop-ups.

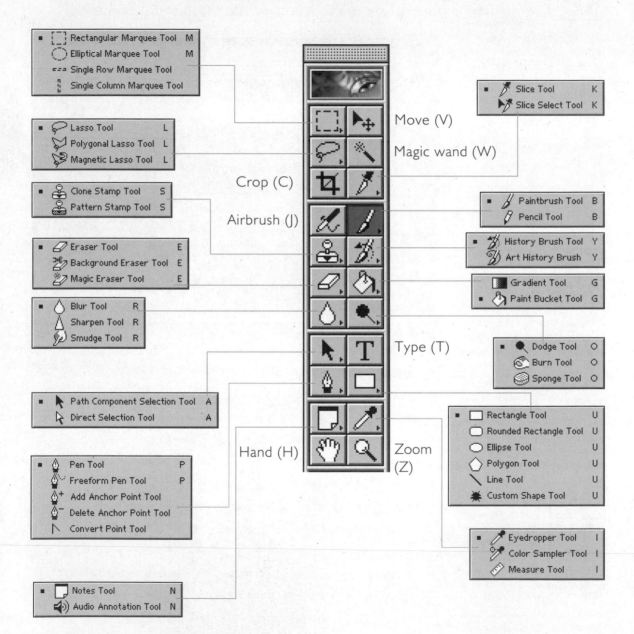

Rectangular Marquee Tool   M
Elliptical Marquee Tool   M
Single Row Marquee Tool
Single Column Marquee Tool

Lasso Tool   L
Polygonal Lasso Tool   L
Magnetic Lasso Tool   L

Clone Stamp Tool   S
Pattern Stamp Tool   S

Eraser Tool   E
Background Eraser Tool   E
Magic Eraser Tool   E

Blur Tool   R
Sharpen Tool   R
Smudge Tool   R

Path Component Selection Tool   A
Direct Selection Tool   A

Pen Tool   P
Freeform Pen Tool   P
Add Anchor Point Tool
Delete Anchor Point Tool
Convert Point Tool

Notes Tool   N
Audio Annotation Tool   N

Move (V)
Magic wand (W)
Crop (C)
Airbrush (J)
Type (T)
Hand (H)
Zoom (Z)

Slice Tool   K
Slice Select Tool   K

Paintbrush Tool   B
Pencil Tool   B

History Brush Tool   Y
Art History Brush   Y

Gradient Tool   G
Paint Bucket Tool   G

Dodge Tool   O
Burn Tool   O
Sponge Tool   O

Rectangle Tool   U
Rounded Rectangle Tool   U
Ellipse Tool   U
Polygon Tool   U
Line Tool   U
Custom Shape Tool   U

Eyedropper Tool   I
Color Sampler Tool   I
Measure Tool   I

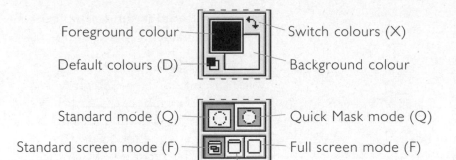

Foreground colour — Switch colours (X)

Default colours (D) — Background colour

Standard mode (Q) — Quick Mask mode (Q)

Standard screen mode (F) — Full screen mode (F)

Full screen mode with menu bar (F)

Jump To button —

Double-click on a tool to show the Options bar for that tool if it is not already showing.

1 Press the keyboard shortcut (in brackets) to access tools.

2 Click and hold on any tool with a small triangle in the bottom right corner to see all tools in that tool group.

When you select a tool in the Toolbox, the Options Bar, extending across the top of the Photoshop window, updates according to the tool you select. Get into the habit of checking these settings before you proceed to use the tool.

3 Hold down Alt and click on any tool in a tool group to cycle through the available tools. Alternatively, hold down Shift, then press the keyboard shortcut for that tool group a number of times. For example, press 'O' three times to cycle through all the tools in the Dodge tool group.

4 Press Tab to hide/show all palettes, including the toolbox. Hold down Shift, then press the Tab key to hide/show all palettes except the Toolbox.

Use Display & Cursor Preferences in the Edit > Preferences menu to change the default appearance of painting and other Cursors.

5 Press Caps Lock to change painting or brush size cursor to a precise crosshair cursor, which indicates the centre of the painting tool. Press Caps Lock again to return to standard cursor display.

Document and Scratch Sizes

The Sizes Bar is useful for monitoring disk space and memory considerations as you work on your images.

Document Sizes

With Document Sizes selected, you will see two numbers separated by a slash. The first number is the size of the image when all layers are flattened. The second number may be larger and represents the file storage size, whilst the image contains additional layers

and/or alpha channels you may have set up. In images that consist of only a single layer, with no additional channels, both numbers are the same.

Scratch Sizes

Use the Plug-ins & Scratch Disk preferences (Edit > Preferences > Plug-Ins & Scratch Disks) to specify the hard disk you want Photoshop to use as a Scratch disk.

The Scratch disk is an underlying technical detail that you should be aware of when using Photoshop. The Scratch disk is a designated hard disk that Photoshop utilises as 'virtual' memory if it runs out of memory (RAM) whilst working on one or more images.

With Scratch Sizes selected in the Sizes Bar you again see two numbers separated by a slash. The first number represents the

amount of memory (RAM) Photoshop needs to handle all currently open pictures. The second number represents the actual amount of memory available to Photoshop. When the first number is greater than the second, Photoshop is using the Scratch disk as virtual memory.

As a general rule of thumb when working in Photoshop, you should have free disk space of at least 3–5 times the file size of the image you are working on. This is because Photoshop makes use of the Scratch disk as virtual memory and because Photoshop needs to hold more than one copy of the image you are working on for the Undo, Revert and History palette functions.

Ruler Guides and Grids

You can show a grid in your image window to help with alignment and measuring, and you can also drag in ruler guides from the rulers. Both sets of guides are non-printing. Customise the appearance of the grid and guides using Edit > Preferences > Guides & Grid.

Make sure that Snap to Guides is selected in the View menu if you want cursors and selections to snap to guides and the grid. This is very useful for aligning elements accurately.

Use keyboard shortcuts: Command/ Ctrl+' to Hide/ Show ruler guides; Command/Ctrl+Alt+' to Hide/Show the grid.

Take care when repositioning ruler guides that you don't reposition the entire background layer accidentally. Make sure you see the bi-directional arrows which indicate that you are dragging a guide.

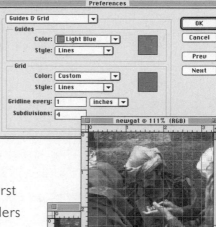

1 To hide or show the grid, choose View > Show / Hide Grid.

2 To create a ruler guide, first choose View > Show Rulers to display the rulers along the top and left edges of the image window. Position your cursor in a ruler and then click and drag onto your image to create either a vertical or horizontal guide.

3 To reposition a ruler guide, select the Move tool, position your cursor on a guide, then click and drag. The cursor changes to a bi-directional arrow when you pick up a guide. To remove a ruler guide, drag the ruler guide back into the ruler it came from. Alternatively, choose View > Clear Guides to remove all guides.

4 To temporarily hide any grid or guides in order to preview the image without the clutter of non-printing guides, choose View Show Extras (Command/Ctrl+H). Use the same command to bring back the guides and grid.

Moving Around

Use any combination of the Navigator palette, the Zoom tool, the Hand tool and the scroll bars for moving around and zooming in and out of your image.

Hold down Command/Ctrl and the Spacebar to temporarily access the Zoom tool with any other tool selected. Add the Alt key to the above combination to zoom out.

With any other tool selected, hold down the Spacebar to temporarily access the Hand tool.

1 Choose Window > Show Navigator to show the Navigator palette. In the palette, you can double-click the % entry box, enter a zoom % (0.29 – 1600%), then press Return/Enter. Alternatively, drag the zoom slider to the right to zoom in, or to the left to zoom out. Each time you change your zoom level, the view in the Preview area updates.

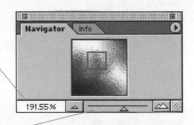

2 Drag the red View box in the Preview area to move quickly to different areas of your image.

3 To use the Zoom tool, select it, position your cursor on the image and click to zoom in on the area around your cursor, in preset increments. With the Zoom tool selected, hold down Alt. The cursor changes to the zoom out cursor; click to zoom out in the preset increments.

4 With the Zoom tool selected, you can also click and drag to define the area you want to zoom in on.

5 You can use the Hand tool in addition to using the scroll bars to move around your image when you have zoomed in on it. Select the tool, position your cursor on the image, then click and drag to reposition.

The Info Palette

The Info palette (Window > Show Info) provides useful numerical read-outs relative to the position of the cursor on your image.

An exclamation mark next to the CMYK readouts indicates that a colour is outside the printable CMYK gamut or range of colours.

You can use it as an on-screen densitometer to examine colour values at the cursor. There are two colour read-outs. As a default, the first colour read-out is the actual colour under the cursor. For example, a read-out of red, green, and blue colour components in an RGB image. The default second read-out is for cyan, magenta, yellow and black values.

The palette also displays x and y coordinates, giving the precise location of the cursor as it moves over the image.

If you create a selection, there is a read-out of the width and height of the selection. The palette also displays values for some options such as rotating, skewing and scaling selections.

| To change the default settings for the Info Palette, choose Palette Options from the pop-up menu.

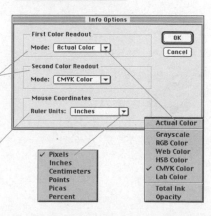

2 Use the Mode pop-ups to choose the first and second colour read-outs.

3 You can also choose a unit of measurement for mouse coordinates.

Palette Techniques

There are twelve floating palettes in Photoshop, (not including the Toolbox or the Options Bar). These movable palettes appear in front of images. Initially the palettes are grouped together.

1 You can show any of the palette groups by selecting the appropriate palette from the Window menu. To close a palette, click on the Close box (Mac) or Close icon (Windows) in the title bar of each palette.

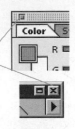

This page uses Macintosh and Windows screen shots to illustrate the degree of similarity in functionality between the Windows and Macintosh platforms.

2 To move a palette, simply position your cursor in the title bar, then click and drag.

3 To choose a particular palette, click on the appropriate tab just below the title bar. You can drag these tabs to create separate palettes. Alternatively, you can drag a tab into another palette to create your own custom groupings of palettes.

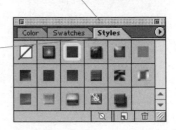

Choose Window > Reset palette locations to recreate the default arrangement of Photoshop's palettes.

4 You can shrink or roll up palettes to make the most of your available screen space. Click the Zoom box (Mac) or Minimise icon (Windows) in the title bar of the palette. Repeat the procedure to restore the palette to its original size. (You have to click twice on the Zoom/Minimise icon if the palette has been resized.)

Double-click a palette tab to collapse the palette to its tab and title bar only. Double-click the tab again to restore it to its previous size.

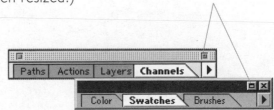

...cont'd

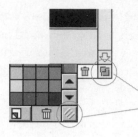

5 You can use standard Macintosh and Windows techniques to resize the Swatches, Navigator, Layers, Channels, Actions and Paths palettes by dragging.

6 You can restore the default settings for all tools by choosing Edit > Preferences > General, then clicking the Reset All Tools button. Alternatively, access the Reset pop-up menu by pressing on the tool icon in the Options bar.

Press the Tab key to hide/ show all palettes including the Toolbox. Hold down Shift, then press Tab to hide/show currently visible palettes, with the exception of the Toolbox.

7 All palettes have a pop-up menu for accessing a range of commands or options relevant to the palette. Click the triangle to access the pop-up menu.

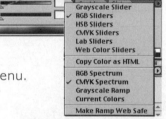

8 At screen resolutions greater than 800x600, the Options bar has a palette docking area on the right hand side. Drag a palette tab into the docking area to create a drop down palette. Click on the palette tab to access the palette. Click on the triangle in the palette tab to access the pop-up menu for the

palette. After making changes to settings in a palette, it collapses back into the docking well when you perform another action on the image. Drag the palette out of the docking well to revert the palette to a standard floating palette.

Saving and Loading Custom Settings

When you save settings, you are creating an independent file which stores the custom information.

It's a good idea to set up a folder within your Adobe folder, or any other appropriate location, for saving your own custom settings. This means you will always be able to access and load the settings quickly and conveniently whenever you need them.

Look in the Presets folder, within the Adobe Photoshop folder, for brush presets that come with Photoshop. Try the Assorted Brushes folder as a starting point for experimenting with different brush types.

Choose Reset Brushes in the pop-up menu to restore settings to their original defaults.

The Swatches, Styles and Actions palettes, the Brushes presets, along with dialogue boxes such as Duotones, Levels and Curves, have Save and Load options which allow you to save custom settings made in the palette or dialogue box and then load them into the same image, or into other Photoshop images. The following example uses the Brushes preset.

1 After creating a custom brush (see pages 70–71), choose Save Brushes in the pop-up menu (in a dialogue box, click the Save button).

2 The Save Brushes In dialogue box prompts you for a file name and location in which to save the settings. The default Brushes folder is in the Presets folder within the Adobe Photoshop folder. The extension for a brushes file is .abr . Make sure you save the file with the correct extension.

3 To load previously saved settings, choose Replace Brushes/ Load Brushes in the pop-up (in a dialogue box click the Load Button), then specify the location of the settings you previously saved. Click on the name, then click Open. Load Brushes adds the new brushes to the existing brushes in the palette. Replace Brushes replaces the current brushes with the new set.

Printing Composites – Mac

A composite image is an image which has not been colour separated and can be useful for low-cost, basic proofing purposes. In a black-and-white laser printer composite, you get a complete image on one sheet of paper, with all colour values converted to shades of grey.

Page Setup

The appearance of the Page Setup dialogue box varies according to the printer selected. Non-PostScript printers do not offer a complete set of options.

1 To print a composite image, first use the Chooser to select the printer you want to use.

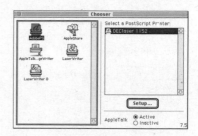

2 Choose File > Page Setup. Make sure the correct printer is selected from the 'Format for' pop-up. From the Paper pop-up, choose the actual

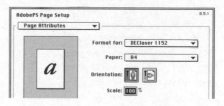

physical size of the paper in your printer onto which you want to print. You can enter a Scale % entry box to increase/decrease the size of the image that prints. Use the Orientation buttons to control the orientation of the image.

3 Choose Adobe Photoshop from the pop-up to specify Photoshop print options. Click the Screen button to change the size, angle and shape of the halftone screen dots. This can be useful for creating special effects. Click the Transfer button to map brightness values in an image to different shades when printed. Background and Border are useful when printing slides. Use Bleed to print outside the 'imageable' area of the page when outputting to an imagesetter.

...cont'd

4 Choose PostScript Options from the pop-up to set further PostScript options if required.

Printing the image

Choose File > Image Info and enter a caption if you want a caption to print with the image.

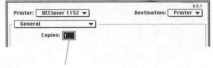

1 Choose File > Print. With General selected, make sure you have the correct printer chosen in the Printer pop-up. Enter the number of copies you want to print.

2 Choose Adobe Photoshop from the pop-up. Check that encoding is set to Binary. This is a more compact and quicker format for sending image data than ASCII. Make sure that Space is set to Greyscale. Click the Print button when you are satisfied with the settings.

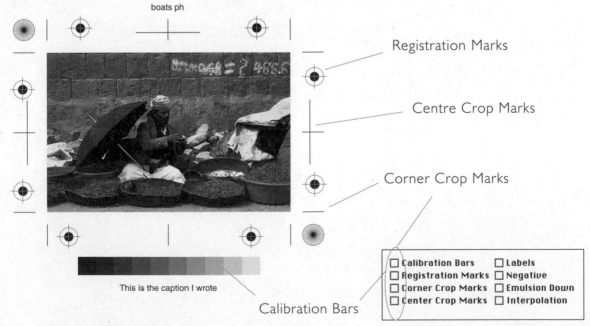

boats ph

Registration Marks

Centre Crop Marks

Corner Crop Marks

This is the caption I wrote

Calibration Bars

☐ Calibration Bars ☐ Labels
☐ Registration Marks ☐ Negative
☐ Corner Crop Marks ☐ Emulsion Down
☐ Center Crop Marks ☐ Interpolation

Printing Composites – Windows

A composite image is an image which has not been colour separated and can be useful for low-cost, basic proofing purposes. In a black and white laser printer composite, you get a complete image, with all colour values converted to shades of grey.

In the Page Setup dialogue box, click the Properties button to set controls specific to your printer. Refer to the manufacturer's manual for information on the options available.

You can choose File > Print, then click the Setup button to go into the Page Setup Dialogue box.

1 To print a composite proof, choose File > Page Setup. Select the printer you want to print to. Check that Paper Size and Orientation are correct. Click the check boxes for calibration bars and registration marks as required. OK the dialogue box.

2 Choose File > Print. Choose a Print Quality from the pop-up. Enter the number of copies you want to print. Some options are available only if you are printing to a PostScript printer. Select the Print As and Encoding options, then click OK. (Binary encoding is a quick, efficient method of encoding image data; ASCII encoding results in a larger, plain-text file, but offers greater compatibility when moving files to and from the Windows platform. JPEG can only be used with PostScript Level 2 printers.)

The History Palette

Every time you modify your image this is recorded in the History palette as a history state. The History palette records the last 20 states of the image.

Once you close an image, all recorded history states and snapshots are discarded.

Use the History palette to return to a previous state of the image within the current work session. The most recent state of the image appears at the bottom of the list in the palette. Each state indicates the name of the tool or command used on the image.

1 To return to a previous state of the image, make sure that the History palette is showing.

You can still use Edit > Undo to undo the last operation. In effect this steps you back one state in the History palette.

2 Click on a state in the History palette. The image reverts to that stage of the work session. States after the state you click on are dimmed. These subsequent states will be discarded if you continue to work from the selected state.

Use File > Revert to revert to the state of your image as it was when you last did a File > Save. The History palette is cleared of all previous history states when you use the Revert command.

3 Alternatively, drag the state slider up or down to indicate the state you wish to move to. Or, choose Step Forward/Step Backward from the pop-up menu in the History palette or from the Edit menu to move sequentially through the states. You can also use the keyboard shortcuts Command/Ctrl+Shift+Z to move to the next state. Use Command+Alt+Z to move to the previous state.

Deleting, Clearing & Purging States

There are three essential techniques for controlling the states listed in the History palette.

Both techniques for deleting states delete the selected state and all states that occur after it. In other words, you are reverting to the state of the image previous to the state you delete.

Deleting States

You can delete states from the History palette to remove the changes to the image recorded by that state and all subsequent states.

1 To delete a history state, click on the name of the state, then choose Delete from the pop-up menu in the History palette.

2 Alternatively, drag the state into the Wastebasket icon at the bottom of the palette.

Clearing States

Clearing states leaves the image at its current state, but removes all previous states from the History palette.

To clear the History palette, use the pop-up menu to choose Clear History. All recorded states are deleted from the History palette, leaving the image at its most recent state.

Purging States

Purging states is useful if you get a low memory message. This is typically because the Undo buffer is becoming full with the changes to the image that it is having to record. When you purge states they are deleted from the Undo buffer, freeing up memory.

You cannot undo the Purge states commands.

1 To purge states, hold down Alt, then choose Clear History from the pop-up menu in the History palette. This command purges history states from the active image.

2 Choose Edit > Purge Histories if you want to purge all history states for all open images.

Taking Snapshots

By default the History palette records the result of the last 20 operations performed on an image. Older states of the image are automatically deleted to keep memory free for Photoshop. You can keep particular states of an image during a work session by taking a 'snapshot' of the image.

A snapshot is created by default when you open an image. This appears at the top of the History palette.

1   To create additional snapshots, click on any state in the History palette.

2   Choose New Snapshot from the pop-up menu in the History palette. In the New Snapshot dialogue box enter a name. OK the dialogue box. A new snapshot is added in the top section of the History palette.

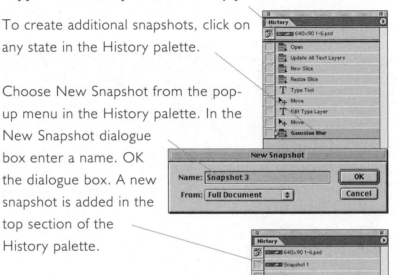

Snapshots exist for the current work session only. When you close an image, all snapshots are lost.

3   Click on a snapshot to revert to the state of the image when the snapshot was created. If you select a snapshot, then continue to work on the image, all history states are lost.

4   To delete a snapshot, click once on the snapshot to select it, then click on the Wastebasket icon at the bottom of the palette.

5   To rename a snapshot, double-click the snapshot name. Enter a name for the snapshot, then click OK.

Opening and Saving Files

Adobe Photoshop began life with the primary purpose of converting image formats for use on different applications and platforms. Since then it has gone on to become a market-leading image-editing application. This chapter covers the basic techniques of opening and saving images in Photoshop.

Covers

Chapter Three

Opening Images in Photoshop

Once you have launched Photoshop you can open images using the File menu. Some specialist file formats open using the File > Import command.

1 To open a picture from within Photoshop, choose File > Open. This takes you into the Open File dialogue box. Navigate through folders and sub-folders as necessary to locate the file you wish to open, click on the file name to select it, then click Open. Alternatively, just double-click the file name.

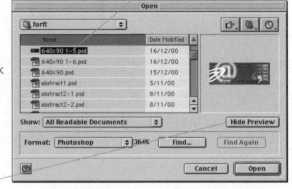

Double-click Photoshop file icons in the Windows or Macintosh file-management environments to open the file. If Photoshop is not running, this will also launch Photoshop.

2 Click the Hide/ Show Preview to hide or to show the thumbnail area to the right of the dialogue box. Select the Show All Readable Documents (Mac), or choose All Formats from the Files of Type pop-up (Windows), to show all files in the selected folder.

Choose Edit > Preferences > Saving Files, then enter a number for Recent File List Contains to control the number of files that appear in the Recent files sub-menu.

3 You can also open recently opened files by choosing File > Open > Recent. Select a file from the list.

640x90 1-5.psd
640x90 1-7.psd
640x90 1-6.psd
svbrshdb.tif

4 To search for a file that you want to open from within the Open dialogue box, click the Find button (Mac). Enter the file name, then click Find/Find Again, until you find the file.

Find: rtcol1

Cancel   Find

Scanning into Photoshop

You can scan into Photoshop either using the TWAIN interface, or using a scanner plug-in designed for use with Photoshop. If your scanner does not have a plug-in for Photoshop, you can use the scanner software to scan the image, save the image in TIFF, PICT or BMP format, then open the file in Photoshop.

 Make sure the plug-in for your scanner is in Photoshop's Import/Export plug-ins folder. Plug-in modules for installed scanners appear in the File > Import sub-menu.

1 To create a scan from within Photoshop, choose File > Import, then select the appropriate device from the sub-menu, or;

2 Choose File > Import > Twain Acquire. This takes you into your scanning software.

 The first time you scan into Photoshop or ImageReady using the TWAIN interface, or when you want to change the image capture device, choose File > Import > TWAIN Select. Select the appropriate icon for your scanner or digital camera, and click OK to specify the device.

Refer to your scanning software manual for details of the controls available. Typically, you can choose settings for scan mode (greyscale, colour, line art etc.), resolution, scale, contrast, brightness and gamma settings.

Many of the scanning controls have equivalent functions in Photoshop. Scanning options vary from scanner to scanner, but you should be able to specify whether you are scanning a transparency or a photograph. The other essential decisions you need to make at this stage are mode, resolution and scale. You will also need to specify a crop area in the preview window.

3 Click the scan button. Wait until the scanning process finishes and the image appears in an untitled Photoshop window. Save the image.

Opening Photo CD Images

Photo CD files are found inside the Images folder within the Photo CD folder.

The Photo CD format, developed by Kodak, and using the YCC colour model, is becoming a more and more popular method for creating and storing digital images. The YCC colour model provides an extremely broad range of colour. The Kodak Precision Color Management System (KPCMS) lets you control the colour mode and display of Photo CD images by specifying profiles for the source film and the destination output device.

1 To open a Photo CD Image, choose File > Open. Select the image you want to open and click OK. The Photo CD Plug-in dialogue box appears.

The Kodak Precision Color Management System is automatically installed on your system when you install Photoshop.

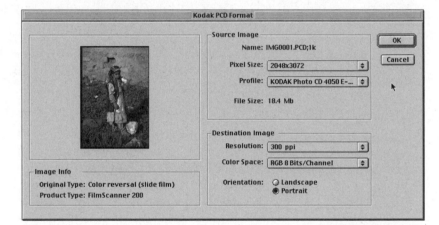

2 Use the Pixel Size pop-up menu to choose a resolution from 128 x 192 pixels (72k, 2.667 by 1.778 inches) to 2,048 x 3,072 pixels (18Mb, 42.668 by 28.445 inches). In this case, resolution refers to the dimensions of the image in pixels.

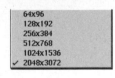

A product type of 052/55 denotes Universal Ektachrome, while 116/22 denotes Universal Kodachrome.

3 The Image Info area of the dialogue box gives information about the image and the medium of the original. This information helps you select the appropriate Precision Transform for a specific Photo CD image.

Profiles are stored in the System\ Preferences\ ColorSync Profiles folder (Mac); the Windows\System \Colour folder (Windows). You may have to obtain the correct profiles before you can select them. (See page 16–17 for further information.)

4 In the Source Image area, use the Profile pop-up menu to choose a suitable profile. The profile you choose needs to match, if possible, the attributes of the Original Type indicated in the Image Info area. In this example the choice is Universal Ektachrome. If the Medium of Original is Colour Reversal, but you don't know the film type, you can use Universal Kodachrome (Universal-E).

Source Image
Name: IMG0001.PCD;1k
Pixel Size: 2048x3072
Profile: KODAK Photo CD 4050 E-...
File Size: 18.4 Mb

✓ KODAK Photo CD 4050 E-6 V3.4
KODAK Photo CD 4050 K-14 V3.4
KODAK Photo CD Color Negative V3.0
KODAK Photo CD Universal E-6 V3.2
KODAK Photo CD Universal K-14 V3.2
Std Photo YCC Print

5 In the Destination Image area, specify the resolution at which you want to open the image. The Pixel Size of the image and the Resolution settings will determine the physical print size of the image when it opens in Photoshop.

Destination Image
Resolution: 300 ppi
Color Space: RGB 8 Bits/Channel
Orientation: ○ Landscape
● P

72 ppi
150 ppi
200 ppi
250 ppi
✓ 300 ppi
350 ppi
400 ppi
450 ppi
500 ppi
550 ppi

6 Select a Colour Space. Typically this will be RGB 8-bits per channel. OK the dialogue box.

✓ RGB 8 Bits/Channel
RGB 16 Bits/Channel
LAB 8 Bits/Channel
LAB 16 Bits/Channel

7 OK the Photo CD Plug-in dialogue box. The image will open in Photoshop.

Opening an EPS File

EPS files, created in applications such as Adobe Illustrator and Macromedia FreeHand, usually contain object-oriented or 'vector' format information. When you open an EPS file in Photoshop, it is rasterised: that is, the vector information is converted into Photoshop's pixel-based format.

1 To open an EPS file as a new document, choose File > Open. Locate and highlight an EPS picture to be opened, then click the Open button. Alternatively, double-click the file name.

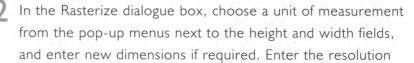

To turn off Anti-aliasing when you open an EPS file in ImageReady, choose Edit > Preferences > General. Deselect the Anti-alias Postscript option.

2 In the Rasterize dialogue box, choose a unit of measurement from the pop-up menus next to the height and width fields, and enter new dimensions if required. Enter the resolution required for your final output device and choose an image mode from the Mode pop-up menu.

3 Select the Constrain Proportions box to keep the original proportions of the EPS. Select Anti-aliased to slightly blur pixels along edges to avoid unwanted jagged edges. Click OK. The EPS appears in its own image window. It is now a bitmap image.

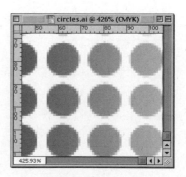

Placing an EPS File

Before you place an EPS into Photoshop, it's a good idea to choose Edit > Preferences > General, then select the Anti-alias PostScript option. This preference helps create a smooth result.

You can also 'place' an Illustrator or FreeHand EPS file into an open Photoshop document. Placed EPS files are automatically placed on a new layer.

1 To place an EPS file into an existing Photoshop file, first open an image in Photoshop, or create a new document.

2 Choose File > Place. Use the Place Document dialogue box to specify the location and name of the EPS file, then click Place.

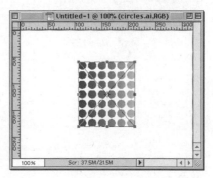

Before you accept the placed EPS, you can also use the Options bar to change position, size, rotation and skew values numerically for the file.

3 A bounding box with eight 'handles' and a cross through the placed image will appear in the Photoshop image window. The EPS image itself may take a few seconds to draw inside the bounding box.

4 If necessary, drag a corner handle to resize the placed image. Hold down Shift as you drag to maintain proportions. Position your cursor inside the bounding box of the placed image and drag to reposition the image.

If you don't want to accept the placed image, with the bounding box still visible, press the Esc key. If you have already placed the image you will have to delete the new layer. (See page 116–117.)

5 When you are satisfied, press Return/Enter, double-click inside the bounding box, or click the OK button in the Options bar. The rasterised file is placed on a new layer.

Saving Files

To create a thumbnail icon that will display in the thumbnail area of the Open dialogue box, choose File > Preferences > Saving Files. Select Always Save from the Image Previews pop-up, then click the Thumbnail option.

The basic principles of saving files in Photoshop – using 'Save' and 'Save As' – are the same as in any other Macintosh or Windows application. Save regularly as you make changes to an image so that you do not lose changes you have made should a system crash occur. You should use Save As to save a new file in the first instance, to make copies of a file, to save a file to a new location and when you need to save an image in a different file format.

Photoshop supports numerous file formats for opening and saving images. Typically, you save an image in a particular format to meet specific output or printing specifications, to compress the image to save disk space, or to open or import the image into an application that requires a particular file format.

Using the Save and Save As commands in ImageReady always saves a file in Photoshop (PSD) file format.

I   To save an image in the first instance, choose File > Save As. Specify where you want to save the file. Enter a name for the file. Use the Format pop-up to choose an appropriate format. Click the Save button. File extensions are added automatically.

2   To save changes as you work on an image, choose File >Save. The previously saved file information is updated.

Photoshop Format

Sometimes referred to as native format: use this format as you work on your image. Applications such as QuarkXPress will not import images in Photoshop format, but all of Photoshop's options, in particular layers, remain available to you in this format. Photoshop also performs open and save routines more quickly when using its native format.

To create image icons for the Finder on the Macintosh, choose Edit > Preferences > Saving Files. Select Always Save from the Image Previews pop-up, then click the Icon option.

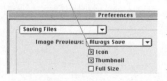

TIFF Format

TIFF (Tagged Image File Format), originally developed by Aldus, became a standard file format for scanned images in the early days of desktop publishing. It is common on both Mac and Windows platforms and is usable in most paint, image-editing and page layout applications.

1   To save an image in TIFF format, choose File > Save As. The Save As dialogue box appears.

On the Macintosh, use the Saving Files Preferences dialogue box to specify whether or not you want file extensions – e.g. '.tif – automatically added when saving files.

Append File Extension: [Ask When Saving ▼]

2   Specify where you want to save the image and enter a name in the name entry box. Use the Format pop-up menu to choose TIFF, then click OK.

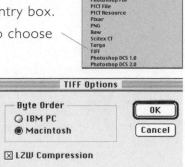

3   The TIFF Options dialogue box will appear. Select Byte Order options and LZW Compression as required, then OK the dialogue box.

Some applications cannot open or import files saved with JPEG or Zip compression.

Byte Order

Use this option to specify whether you want the TIFF to be used on a Mac or a PC, as Mac and PC TIFF formats vary slightly.

LZW Compression

A warning appears at the bottom of the Save As dialogue box if an image uses features, such as layers or alpha channels, that are not supported by that particular file format.

(Lempel-Ziv-Welch) is a compression format that looks for repeated elements in the computer code that describes the image and replaces these with shorter sequences. It is a 'lossless' compression scheme - none of the image's detail is lost. Applications such as QuarkXPress, Adobe PageMaker, Adobe InDesign and Macromedia FreeHand can import TIFFs with LZW compression.

⚠ Some of the document's data will not be saved using the chosen format and options.

Photoshop EPS

EPS is generally more reliable for PostScript printing than the TIFF file format, but generates file sizes which can be three to four times greater than TIFFs with LZW compression. To save in EPS format, do the following:

Follow the procedure for saving TIFFs, but choose Photoshop EPS from the Format pop-up menu. Click OK. The EPS Options dialogue box will appear. Specify your settings, then click OK.

Preview

This option specifies the quality of the low-resolution screen preview you see when you import the image into applications such as Adobe PageMaker and QuarkXPress. Use 'Macintosh (8bits/pixel)' for a colour preview. 'Macintosh (JPEG)' uses JPEG compression routines, but is only supported by Postscript Level 2 printers. Use TIFF if you want to use the image in Windows.

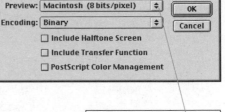

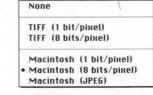

Encoding

Use binary encoding if you want to export the image for use with Adobe Illustrator. Some applications do not recognise binary encoding; in this case you have to use ASCII.

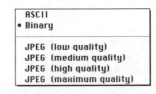

JPEG Format

JPEG is an acronym for Joint Photographic Experts Group. It is an extremely efficient compression format and is frequently used for images on the World Wide Web. JPEG format is available when saving Greyscale, RGB and CMYK images.

The JPEG compression routine is a 'lossy' procedure. To make the file size of the image smaller, image data is discarded, resulting in reduced image quality.

1 Follow the procedure for saving in TIFF format, but choose JPEG from the Format pop-up menu. OK the Save as dialogue box.

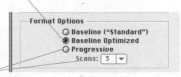

2 Use the Quality pop-up to specify the amount of compression, or drag the slider. Maximum gives best image quality, retaining most of the detail in an image, but results in the least compression. Low gives lowest image quality, but gives maximum compression.

Older browsers cannot display baseline optimised images.

JPEG is a cumulative compression scheme – if you close an image, then reopen it and save it in JPEG format, you will apply a further compression to the image, effectively losing more colour information from the image. Save to JPEG format only after you finish all work on an image.

3 In the Format Options area, select Baseline Optimised to optimise the colour quality of the image.

4 Select Progressive and enter a value for Scans if you'll use the image on the World Wide Web and want the image to download in a series of passes adding detail progressively.

5 The compressed file size is indicated in the Size area. Choose a modem speed from the Size pop-up to see an estimated download time for the image at the specified modem speed.

Creating a New File

When you need a fresh, completely blank canvas to work on, you can create a new file.

Whilst the New dialogue box is active, if you have an image window already open, you can choose the window's name from the bottom of the Window menu; the New dialogue box will update with the settings from the file you selected.

1 To create a new file, choose File > New. Enter a name for the new document (or leave this as Untitled and do a Save As later).

2 Specify width and height settings. If you have copied or cut pixels to the clipboard, the width and height fields automatically reflect the dimensions of the elements on the clipboard.

3 Enter a resolution and choose a colour mode.

4 Select one of the contents options to specify the canvas background you want to begin with, then OK the dialogue box.

You can also use the Fill command to fill selections with colour.

5 To change the colour of the canvas, select a foreground colour (see Chapter Five, 'Defining Colours'). Next, choose Edit > Fill. Choose Foreground from the Use pop-up. Make sure Opacity is set to 100% and Mode is Normal. Click OK.

Getting Started with Images

There are a number of common techniques and tasks, such as cropping an image and making it larger or smaller, or changing the resolution to suit your final output needs, that you need to undertake on many of the images on which you work. This chapter covers a range of these tasks.

Covers

Chapter Four

Rotating an Image

You can quickly rotate an image if you have scanned it at the wrong orientation, or, for example, if you have opened a Photo CD image using the Landscape option.

To rotate an image in set increments, use Image > Rotate Canvas. Choose one of the preset increments. CW stands for clockwise, CCW for counter-clockwise. In the example above, you would choose 90 degrees counter-clockwise to rotate the Beijing Duck seller upright.

When using arbitrary rotation, position a ruler (see page 25, 'Ruler Guides and Grids') to help determine how far you need to rotate.

Sometimes you need to adjust an image a few degrees to make up for a poor original photograph or slightly misaligned scan:

2 To rotate in precise amounts, choose Image > Rotate Canvas > Arbitrary. Enter a value for the rotation. Choose the clockwise (CW) or counter-clockwise (CCW) radio button, then OK the dialogue box.

3 You may need to recrop the image. Use Unsharp mask to compensate for any blurring due to the rotation.

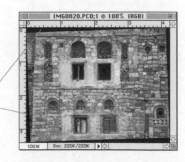

Resizing without Resampling

When you make the image smaller without resampling, the pixels get smaller. Effectively, you are increasing the resolution of the image. When you make an image bigger without resampling, the pixels get larger and this can lead to jagged, blocky results. Effectively, you are reducing the resolution of the image.

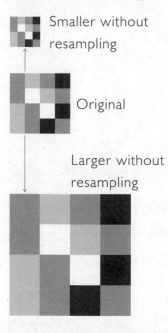

Smaller without resampling

Original

Larger without resampling

When you resize an image without resampling, you make the image larger or smaller without changing the total number of pixels in the image. The overall dimensions of the image change, the file size remains the same, but the resolution of the image goes up if you make the image smaller, down if you make the image larger.

1 To decrease the size of your image without resampling, choose Image > Image Size. Make sure that Resample Image is deselected. Enter a lower value in the Width or Height entry box. The other measurement updates automatically. The file size of the image remains the same – no pixels have been added. The resolution has increased – the same number of pixels are packed into a smaller area.

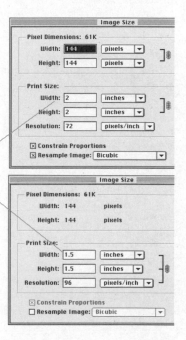

2 To increase the size of your image without resampling, enter a higher value in the Width or Height entry box. The file size of the image remains the same, but the resolution has decreased.

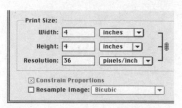

Resampling Up

Resampling up involves interpolation. Interpolation is used when Photoshop has to add information – new pixels – that didn't previously exist to an image. There are three methods to choose from the pop-up in the Image size dialogue box. Bicubic gives best results, but takes longest; Nearest Neighbour is quickest, but least accurate.

When you resample up, new pixels are added to the image, so file size increases. Resampling takes place when you increase the resolution setting, or the width/height setting with the Resample Image option selected.

This example starts with a 2 in by 2 in image at 72 ppi.

As far as possible, try to avoid resampling up. You are adding pixels to the image, without increasing the quality and detail in the image. You get better results if you scan the image at the size at which you intend to use it and at the resolution required for output.

To reset the dialogue box to its original settings, hold down Alt, then click the Reset button.

1   Choose Image > Image Size. To keep the overall dimensions of the image, but increase the resolution, make sure that Resample Image is selected. Select Constrain Proportions so that the image's original proportions are maintained. Enter a higher value in the Resolution box.

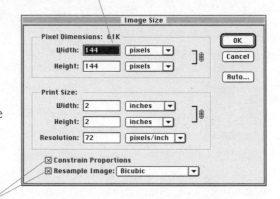

2   The file size and total number of pixels increase, but the width and height dimensions remain the same.

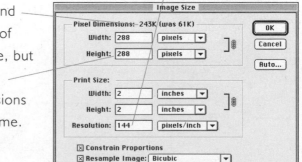

You now have an image which is the same overall size, but which has more pixels in the same area, and therefore its resolution is increased:

When you resample an image, blurring may occur due to the process of interpolation. Use the Unsharp Mask filter to compensate for this. (See page 177.)

3 To make the overall dimensions of the image bigger, but to keep the same resolution, again make sure that Resample Image is selected. Select Constrain Proportions to keep width and height proportional. Enter a higher value in either the Width or Height entry boxes. (The other entry box will update automatically if you have selected Constrain Proportions.)

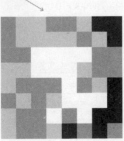

4 The overall dimensions of the image have now increased. The file size and total number of pixels have also increased, but the resolution remains the same.

Sampling Down

You sometimes need to resample down to maintain an optimal balance between the resolution needed for acceptable final output and file size considerations. There is little point in working with an image at too high a resolution if some of the image information is redundant at final output.

Resampling down means discarding pixels. The result is a smaller file size. Resampling down occurs when you decrease the resolution setting, or the width/ height setting with Resample Image option selected.

These examples start with a 2 by 2 inch image at 300 ppi.

Choose View > Print Size to get a representation on screen of the physical size of the image when printed.

1 Choose Image > Image Size. To keep the overall dimensions of the image, but decrease the resolution, make sure that Resample Image is selected. Leave Constrain Proportions selected, so that the image's original proportions are maintained. Reduce the value in the Resolution box.

2 The file size goes down and the total number of pixels decreases, whilst the width and height dimensions remain the same.

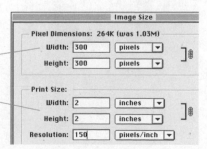

You now have an image which is the same overall size, but with fewer pixels in the same area, and therefore its resolution is decreased:

3 To reduce the overall dimensions of the image, but keep the image at the same resolution, again make sure that Resample Image is selected. (Select Constrain Proportions to keep the width and height proportional.) Enter a lower value in either the width or height entry box. (The other entry box will update automatically if you have selected Constrain Proportions.)

4 The overall dimensions of the image have now decreased. The file size and the total number of pixels have also decreased, but the resolution remains the same.

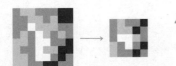

Cropping an Image

Use the Crop tool to crop unwanted areas of an image and reduce the file size.

HOT TIP

Press C on the keyboard to select the Crop tool, then press Return/Enter to show the Crop tool options bar if it not already showing.

1 Select the Crop tool. Position your cursor on the image, then click and drag to define the crop area. Don't worry if you don't get the crop exactly right first time. The area of the image outside the crop dims to indicate the parts of the image that will be discarded.

HOT TIP

With a crop marquee active, use the Shield cropped area option in the Options bar to hide/show the crop shading overlay. You can also change the colour and/or opacity of the crop shading.

Shield cropped area Color: ☐ Opacity: 75% ▶

2 To reposition the crop marquee, place your cursor inside the marquee, then click and drag. To resize the crop marquee, place your cursor on one of the 8 handles around the marquee (the cursor changes to a bi-directional arrow), then click and drag. To rotate the marquee, position your cursor just outside the marquee (the cursor changes shape to indicate rotation), then click and drag in a circular direction.

HOT TIP

Hold down Shift, then click and drag on a corner handle to resize the crop marquee in proportion.

HOT TIP

The Crop tool snaps to the edge of the image. To prevent the snap effect, hold down Command/Ctrl as you create or resize the crop marquee.

3 When you are satisfied with the position and size of the crop marquee, press Return/Enter to crop the picture. Alternatively, you can double-click inside the crop marquee. The areas outside the marquee are discarded. Press the Esc key if you do not want to accept the crop marquee.

Adding a Border

Borders are useful when you need additional space around the edges of your image.

Make sure that you select a background colour for your border, before you use the Canvas Size dialogue box.

1 Choose Image > Canvas Size. Use the measurement pop-up menus to choose a unit of measurement. Enter increased values for the width and/or height fields.

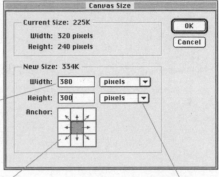

2 To specify where the border is added relative to the image, click one of the white placement squares. This sets the relative position of the image and the border. The grey square represents the position of the image, the white squares the position of the border.

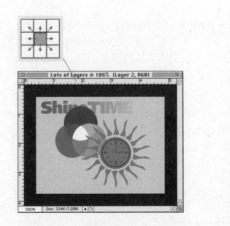

3 OK the dialogue and the border is added, filled with the background colour.

Image Modes

Image modes are fundamental to working in Photoshop. When you open an image the mode is indicated in the title bar of the image window. There are eight different modes in Photoshop. Use modes as appropriate to your working requirements. Then, depending on output or printing requirements, if necessary, convert to a different mode.

RGB Mode

Images are typically scanned or captured in RGB mode. When you start work with a colour image it is usually best to work in RGB mode, as this is faster than CMYK mode and allows you to use all of Photoshop's commands and features, providing greatest flexibility.

The disadvantage of working in RGB mode, if your image will be printed, is that RGB allows a greater gamut of colours than you can print. At some stage, some of the brightest, most vibrant colours may lose their brilliance when the image is brought within the CMYK gamut.

CMYK Mode

Convert to CMYK when the image is to be printed and you have finished making changes.

You can retain the flexibility of working in RGB mode, but see an on-screen CMYK preview of your image, by choosing View > CMYK Preview. (You may have to wait a few seconds when you choose this option as Photoshop builds its colour conversion tables.)

To place a colour image in a page layout application from where it will be colour separated, you need to convert from RGB to CMYK. When you convert from RGB to CMYK, Photoshop adjusts any colours in the RGB image that fall outside the CMYK gamut to their nearest printable colour. (See Chapter Five, 'Defining Colours', for details on gamut warnings.)

You can also select Display out of Gamut colours from the View menu, to highlight (in grey) areas of the image that are out of gamut.

Indexed Colour Mode

This mode reduces your image to 256 colours or less and is frequently used for multimedia and Web images. (See Chapter 15, 'Web and Multimedia Images'.)

You must first convert to greyscale mode before you can convert to Duotone mode.

Duotone

For details on using Duotone mode see the following page.

Greyscale Mode

When you are not printing an image in colour you can convert to greyscale mode to make working faster and file size smaller.

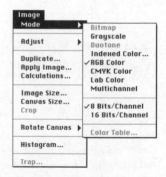

Lab Mode

This mode uses the CIE Lab mode which has one channel for luminosity, an 'a' channel representing colours blue to yellow, a 'b' channel for magenta to green. A significant advantage to this mode is that its gamut encompasses that of both CMYK and RGB modes.

Bitmap Mode

This mode reduces everything to black or white pixels. The image becomes a one-bit image.

To convert from one mode to another, choose Image > Mode and choose the mode you want from the sub-menu. Depending on which mode you are converting from and to, you may get a message box warning you of any consequences of converting to the new mode and asking you to confirm your request.

Duotone Mode

You can only access Duotone mode when you have converted to Greyscale mode.

Duotone is a very popular effect used to give added tonal depth to a greyscale image by printing with black and another colour.

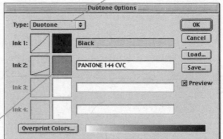

1 To create a duotone, choose Image > Mode > Duotone. Choose from the pop-up whether you want to create a duotone (two inks), a tritone (three inks) or a quadtone (four inks).

When you start working with Photoshop, click on the Load button and try using one of the preset duotone settings that can be found in: Adobe Photoshop > Presets > Duotone Presets > Duotones.

2 To choose a second colour for the duotone, click the 'Ink 2' colour box (below the black ink box). This takes you into the Custom Colours dialogue box. Choose a colour. Click the Picker button if you want to use the Colour Picker. OK the dialogue box.

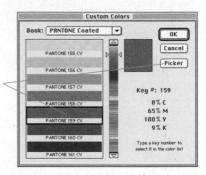

Make sure you save duotones in EPS format so that they colour separate correctly from page layout applications.

3 To specify the ink coverage for both colours, click first on the Ink 1 Curve box, then the Ink 2 box. In the Duotone Curve dialogue box, drag the curve to the desired position, or enter values in the % entry boxes to adjust the ink coverage curve. Click the Preview option to preview the result in the image window before you OK the dialogue boxes.

Defining Colours

Defining colours is an essential aspect of using Photoshop and there is a range of techniques that can be used. The colour controls in the Toolbox indicate the current foreground and background colours.

Covers

Chapter Five

Foreground and Background Colours

The foreground colour is applied when you create type, and when you use the Paint Bucket, Line, Pencil, Airbrush and Paintbrush tools.

The background colour is the colour you erase to when you use the Eraser tool, or when you delete or move a selection.

When you are working with foreground and background controls you can also switch colours, and you can quickly change back to the default colours, black and white.

You can change the background and foreground colours using the Eyedropper tool, the Colour Picker palette, the Colour palette and the Swatches palette.

Press X on the keyboard to switch background and foreground colours. Press D on the keyboard to revert to the default foreground and background colours.

1 To switch background to foreground and vice versa, click once on the Switch Colours arrow.

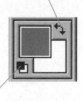

2 To revert to black and white as the default background and foreground colours, click the Default colours icon.

The Eyedropper and Colour Sampler Tools (I)

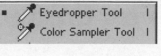

The Eyedropper Tool

The Eyedropper tool provides a quick and convenient way to pick up foreground and background colour from an area of the image you are working on, or from another inactive Photoshop image window.

1 To set the foreground colour, click on the Eyedropper tool. Position your cursor, then click once on the image. (The foreground box in the Toolbox now represents the colour where you clicked.)

2 To set the background colour, hold down Alt, then click on the image. The background box in the Toolbox now indicates the colour on which you clicked.

3 To set the Sample Size, use the Sample Size pop-up menu in the Options bar to choose a value. Point Sample reads the precise value of the pixel on which you click. 3 by 3 and 5 by 5 take average values of the pixels where you click.

The Colour Sampler Tool

Use the Colour Sampler tool (with the Info palette) to set up to four sample points which you can refer to as you make adjustments to colour values. Each time you click in the image window with the Colour Sampler tool, you set a sample point. Each point creates an extra pane in the Info palette. To delete a sample point, drag it out of the image window with the Colour Sampler tool.

To hide/show the sample points, choose Hide/Show Sample Points from the Info palette pop-up.

The Colour Picker Palette

One of the most powerful and flexible ways of choosing foreground and background colours is using the Colour Picker palette. You can use a number of different colour models to create colour.

Press the Tab key to move the highlight through the entry boxes in the dialogue box.

1 To create a Process colour using the Colour Picker, click once on either the foreground or background colour box.

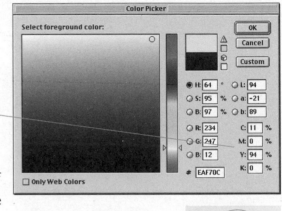

A warning triangle – the Gamut alarm – will appear next to the Current/ Previous colour boxes if you create a colour that cannot be printed using CMYK inks. Click the warning triangle to choose the nearest printable colour. The small box below the warning triangle indicates the nearest printable colour.

2 Enter values in the CMYK entry boxes. You will see a preview of the colour in the Current Colour swatch, above the Previous Colour swatch.

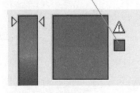

3 OK the dialogue box. The colour you defined now becomes the foreground or background colour, depending on which box you clicked in step 1.

You can also create colours using the Colour Slider and the Colour field. The next example uses Hue, Saturation and Brightness values. Use the same techniques for Red, Green, Blue (RGB) and Lab colour models.

1 To create a colour using Hue, Saturation and Brightness (HSB) values, first click the Hue (H) radio button.

2 Click on the Colour Slider bar, or drag the slider triangles on either side of the bar, to choose a hue or colour. This sets one of the three HSB values. The number in the Hue entry box represents the hue you have chosen (0–360).

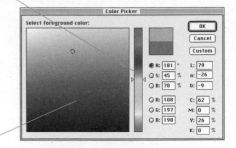

3 Next, click in the Colour Field to set the other two variables – Saturation and Brightness. Clicking to the left of the field reduces the saturation, clicking to the right increases the saturation of the selected hue. Clicking near the bottom decreases brightness, clicking near the top increases brightness for the selected hue.

4 If you click on the Saturation button, the Colour Slider now represents saturation (from 0–100) and the Colour field allows you to choose Hue and Brightness values. When you click the Brightness radio button, the slider represents Brightness and the Colour field represents Hue and Saturation.

If the Web Colours Only option is deselected, the Non-web colour alert appears if you create a colour that is not in the Web palette. Click the Web alert icon to move the colour to the nearest Web-safe colour.

Web-safe Colours

1 To create a Web-safe colour, select the Only Web Colours option. Fewer colours are represented in the Colour Field; each colour exists in the Web palette which consists of 216 colours.

Selecting PANTONE Colours

You can access a range of colour-matching systems using the Colour Picker dialogue box. These include: Toyo Colour Finder 1050 System, Focoltone Colour System, PANTONE Matching System, Trumatch Swatching System and DIC Colour Guide. Here, we'll select a PANTONE colour.

1 To select a PANTONE colour, click the foreground or background colour box. The Colour Picker dialogue box will appear. Click the Custom button.

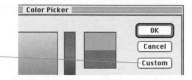

2 Use the Book pop-up menu to select a PANTONE matching system.

In the Custom Colours dialogue box, click the Picker button to return to the Colour Picker dialogue box.

3 If you know the PANTONE number of the colour you want, you can enter the number on the keyboard. Alternatively, click in the colour slider bar to the right of the PANTONE colour boxes. This moves you to a general range of colours. Then click on the scroll bars at the top and bottom of the sliders to find the specific PANTONE colour you want.

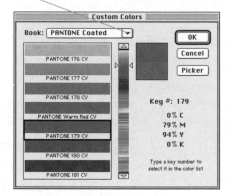

4 Click on the colour you want to select, then click OK.

The Colour Palette

You can also use the Colour palette (Window > Show Colours) to mix new colours.

If you click the active colour selection box, you will display the Colour Picker palette.

1 First identify which colour selection box is 'active'. There are two boxes, foreground and background. The active box is outlined in black.

2 Continue with step 3 if the correct box is active, or click the inactive box to make it the active box if necessary.

During step 3, if you create a colour that is outside the CMYK colour gamut, the gamut alert warning triangle appears. You can click on the alert triangle to set the colour to the nearest CMYK equivalent. The nearest CMYK equivalent appears in a box next to the alert triangle.

3 Drag the colour slider triangles below the colour slider bars, or enter values in the entry boxes to the right of the palette. You can also click on a colour in the Colour Bar running along the bottom of the Colour palette. The Colour Bar contains every colour in the CMYK spectrum as a default setting.

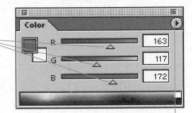

4 Use the pop-up triangle in the top right of the palette to change the colour model for the sliders.

5 Choose an option from the bottom half of the pop-up menu to specify the colour model for the colours in the Colour Bar at the bottom of the palette.

The Swatches Palette

You can use the Swatches palette (Window > Show Swatches) to set foreground and background colours, and you can also use it to create custom palettes which you can save and then reload into a different image.

See page 30 for details on loading and saving custom palette settings.

1 To select a foreground colour from the Swatches palette, click on a colour swatch. To select a background colour, hold down Alt and then click on a colour swatch.

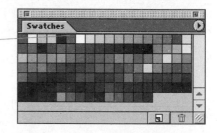

You can customise the Swatches palette by adding and deleting colours in the palette.

Shift-clicking on an existing swatch replaces it with the current foreground colour. Pressing Shift and then Alt while clicking on a swatch inserts the current foreground colour to the left of the colour you click.

2 To add colour to the swatches, select a foreground colour. Position your cursor in an empty area of the Swatches palette. (The cursor changes to a paint bucket.) Then click. Enter a name for the new swatch, then click OK to add the current foreground colour to the Swatches palette.

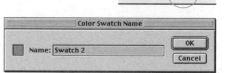

Position your cursor on a swatch in the Swatches palette, hold down Ctrl (Mac), or click the right mouse button (PC) to access the context sensitive menu:

New Swatch...
Rename Swatch...
Delete Swatch

3 To delete a colour swatch, hold down Command (Mac) or Ctrl (Windows) and then click on a colour swatch.

4 Use the Swatches palette pop-up menu to reset the Swatches palette to its default settings, or to choose a different colour palette from the list.

The Painting Tools

The Paintbrush, Airbrush, Pencil, and Line tools apply the foreground colour to pixels in your image as you drag across them. Each painting tool creates a painting stroke with different characteristics. You can use the Brushes palette to determine the shape, size and type of the brush stroke for the Airbrush, Paintbrush, and Pencil tools.

All the painting and editing tools can be used within a selection or directly on an image.

Covers

The Brushes Palette

The Brushes palette is central to using the painting and editing tools. Before you use any of these tools you need to check your brush size and shape. Brush settings are located in the Options bar.

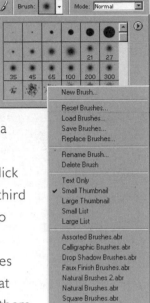

1   To choose a brush for the currently selected painting or editing tool, click the Brush pop-up triangle in the Options bar.

2   To choose a hard-edged brush, click a brush in the first row of the default palette. To use a soft-edged brush, click one of the brushes in the second or third rows. (The circle icons in the first two rows represent the actual size of the brush.) The third row contains brushes that are too large to be represented at their actual size. The number below them is the diameter of the brush in pixels. The remaining brushes create more painterly brush strokes.

3   Click on a brush to select it, then click the pop-up triangle again to close the Brush palette.

4   To create a new brush, choose New Brush from the pop-up menu. Enter values for Diameter, Hardness, Spacing, Angle and Roundness in the New Brush dialogue box. Enter a name for the brush.

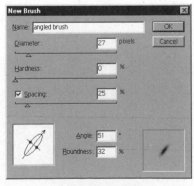

Diameter

Enter a value in pixels for the diameter of your brush from 1–999. Brush sizes too large to be represented at their actual size will display with the diameter indicated as a number.

Hardness

A setting of 100% gives a hard-edged brush. Settings below 100% produce soft-edged brushes. The lower you take this setting, the more diffuse the resultant stroke when you paint with the brush. Even with a setting of 100%, the edge of the brush-stroke is anti-aliased.

Spacing

To edit the settings for a selected brush, click the brush size icon in the options bar.

Spacing is measured as a percentage of brush size. 25% is the default setting for all brushes. Higher settings begin to create non-continuous strokes.

Angle and Roundness

Use these controls together to create a stroke which thickens and thins like a calligraphic pen. You can enter values in the entry boxes, or drag the arrow indicator to change the angle, and drag the diameter dots to change the diameter.

To delete a brush, click on it to select it, then choose Delete Brush in the pop-up menu.

5 OK the dialogue box. The new brush is added to the palette. The new brush is automatically selected. (See page 30 for details on saving customised palettes for future use.)

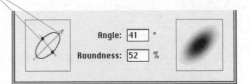

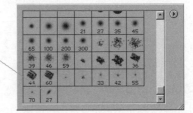

Painting Tool Techniques and Settings

Each painting tool has its own Options bar. There is a range of Options bar settings and techniques common to many of the painting and editing tools. Use the options covered here in conjunction with the specific controls for each of the tools on the following pages.

With a tool selected, press Return/Enter to show the tool Options bar if it is not already showing.

Opacity, Pressure and Exposure

Opacity (Paintbrush, Line, Pencil, Eraser, Rubber Stamp), Pressure (Airbrush, Smudge, Focus tools) and Exposure (Toning tools) have a similar effect and determine the intensity of the tool you are working with. For example, opacity controls how completely pixels are covered by the foreground colour when you drag across them.

Make sure the Opacity/Pressure slider is at 100% if you want to completely cover the pixels you drag across. (Soft-edged brushes only partially cover pixels around the edge of the painting stroke to create the soft edge effect.) Reducing the Opacity/Pressure setting gives less complete results in the area you drag across, creating a semi-transparent, partially-covered effect.

Number keys on the keyboard can be used to set Opacity. With a painting tool selected, type two numbers in quick succession to specify Opacity settings.

Fade

Use the Brush Dynamics pop-up menu, in the right of the Options bar, to vary combinations of size, opacity and colour settings. Choose Fade from the pop-up menus as required, then specify a number of steps to specify how quickly the fade takes place. Higher values fade the effect over a greater distance.

1   To set a fade rate for the currently selected painting or editing tool, make sure the Options bar is showing. Click on the Brush Dynamics pop-up.

2   Choose Fade from the pop-up menus. Enter a value to control how quickly the selected option fades to nothing.

Brush Dynamics		
Size:	Off	steps
Opacity:	Off	steps
Color:	Fade	67 steps

Undoing

To undo the last stroke you painted, choose Edit > Undo. This only works for the very last action you performed. In instances where you need to undo several steps, you can use the History palette. Use File > Revert to revert to the version of the file when you last saved it.

Cursor Types

Press Caps Lock to change painting and editing tool cursors to precise crosshairs. This is a very useful technique for making fine adjustments.

Whilst you are working with a painting tool, hold down Alt to temporarily access the Eyedropper tool. This is useful for selecting a new foreground colour with which to paint.

2 Choose File > Preferences > Display and Cursors to change the way your painting tool cursors appear on-screen. 'Precise' has the same effect as pressing Caps Lock. 'Brush Size' is useful because you see the actual brush size represented on screen. (Changing the Painting Cursors preference to Precise reverses the effect of Caps Lock.)

Select Use All Layers when you want Photoshop to take into account, or 'sample', pixels from layers other than the target layer. In effect, the tool samples pixels from all layers as if they were merged.

Resetting Painting Tool Options

You can use the pop-up menu in each of the painting tool Options bars to reset the default setting for the tool, or you can reset defaults for all tools.

The Paintbrush Tool (B)

The Paintbrush in Photoshop is like a normal paintbrush. You drag it across the pixels in your image and it colours those pixels with the foreground colour.

You can use a Fade setting to make the paint run out, just as with a normal paintbrush. You can change the opacity setting to achieve a translucent, partial coverage of the pixels you drag across. You can also change the Size of the brush so that the brush stroke becomes smaller and smaller as it progresses.

Use the Brush Dynamics pop-up in the Options bar to create settings for Size, Opacity and Colour.

1 To paint with the Paintbrush (B) first select the tool. Use the Brush palette pop-up to choose a brush size and type. (See page 70.)

2 Choose the settings you want, then position your cursor on the image, click and drag.

Wet Edges (Paintbrush & Eraser)

To constrain your painting strokes to straight lines, click with the Painting tool to position the start of the stroke, move your cursor, (do not click and drag), then hold down Shift and click to end the stroke.

When you paint with wet edges selected you get a stroke that is darker around the edges and translucent inside the stroke, imitating the uneven build-up of paint in a watercolour.

Standard   Wet Edges

Fade = 60

The Airbrush Tool (J)

Use the Airbrush tool to imitate the effect of spraying paint with an airbrush. The airbrush paints with the foreground colour.

For a description of blending modes see pages 80–81.

1 To paint with the Airbrush tool (J), first select the tool. Use the Brushes pop-up palette to specify a size and type for the brush. Use a soft-edged brush to create the most realistic airbrush effect. Set options for Blending Mode and Pressure. Use the Brush Dynamics pop-up to create settings for Size, Pressure and Colour.

To change the Pressure setting using the keyboard, type numbers on the keyboard. For example, type 7 to specify a Pressure setting of 70%. Type 7 then 8 in quick succession to create a setting of 78%.

2 Click and drag across the image to apply the foreground colour. The more you spray over an area, the greater the build-up of colour. The speed at which you drag the airbrush also affects the intensity of the paint.

The Pencil (N) and Line (U) Tools

The Pencil Tool (N)

You can use the Pencil tool to draw freeform lines. The lines you draw with the Pencil tool are always hard-edged – in other words, the edges of your lines are not anti-aliased. The Pencil tool paints or draws with the foreground colour.

Use the Brushes palette to specify the size of your pencil.

1 To draw a line, first select the Pencil tool. Set a brush size using the Brushes pop-up palette. Use the Pencil Options bar to specify: Blending Mode, Opacity, and Auto Erase options.

2 Use the Brush Dynamics pop-up to set Fade options for Size, Opacity and Colour if required.

3 Click and drag to create a freeform pencil stroke. Click, hold down Shift, then drag to constrain the pencil stroke vertically or horizontally. Click, move the cursor to a new position (do not click and drag), hold down Shift, then click again to create a straight pencil stroke between the two points.

Auto Erase

Select this option to use the Pencil tool as an eraser.

The Line Tool (U)

Use the Line tool to create straight lines. Lines are filled with the foreground colour. Lines are always hard-edged.

You cannot specify a brush size for the Line tool; use the Line Width setting in the Line Tool Options bar instead.

1 To draw a straight line select the Line tool to show the Line Tool Options bar. Set options for creating a rasterised shape or a new shape layer, (see pages 83–84). Specify a line weight, blending mode and opacity.

2 Click and drag on the image to create a line. You can hold down Shift as you click and drag to constrain the line to 45-degree increments.

You must specify arrowhead settings before you create a line.

3 To add arrowheads to the beginning or end of a line, click the Start/End options as appropriate. Click the Shape button to define the shape of the arrowhead.

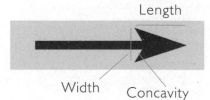

Depending on the option you choose in the Options bar, the Line tool can be used to create either a rasterised shape, or a new shape layer. (See pages 83–84.)

4 Enter Width, Length and Concavity settings. OK the dialogue box, then click and drag to create the line.

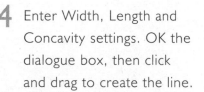

Length

Width   Concavity

The Length and Width settings for an arrowhead are specified as a percentage of the line weight.

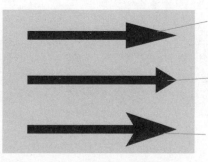

Width = 300, Length = 600, Concavity = 0

Width = 300, Length = 250, Concavity = 0

Width = 300, Length = 600, Concavity = 20

The Gradient Tool (G)

You can use the Gradient tool to create transitions from one colour to another. You can also create multi-coloured gradients. There are options for Linear, Radial, Angle, Reflected and Diamond gradients. You can apply a gradient fill to a selection, or to an entire active layer.

1   To create a gradient fill, select the Gradient tool. Choose a gradient type from the Options bar.

Hold down Shift as you click and drag to constrain a linear gradient to 45-degree increments.

2   Select a Blending mode and set Opacity. Use the gradient pop-up to choose from one of the preset gradients.

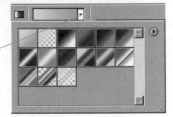

For a linear gradient, the start and end colours fill any part of the selection that you do not drag the cursor across. For radial gradients, the end colour fills the remaining area.

3   Position your cursor where you want the gradient to start, then click and drag. The angle and distance you drag the cursor defines the angle and distance of a linear gradient, or the radius of a radial gradient. (Click and drag from the centre out to create Radial, Angle, Reflected and Diamond gradient fills.)

4   For basic gradient fills leave the Transparency and Dither options selected.

Linear   Radial   Angle   Reflected   Diamond

The Paint Bucket Tool (G)

You can use the Paint Bucket tool to colour pixels with the foreground colour, based on a tolerance setting. It works in a similar way to the Magic Wand tool, but in this case, filling adjoining pixels that fall within the tolerance setting. You can use the Paint Bucket tool within a selection or on the entire image.

1 To fill an area with the foreground colour, select the Paint Bucket tool. Leave the Fill pop-up set to Fill. Enter a value from 0–255 in the Tolerance box. The higher you set the value, the greater the pixel range the Paint Bucket will fill.

The Anti-aliased option creates a slightly soft edge on the areas that the Paint Bucket fills.

2 Set Opacity, Blending mode, Anti-aliased and All Layers options. Position your cursor then click on the image.

3 You can use the Paint Bucket to fill with a pattern previously saved into the pattern buffer. Use the Fill pop-up to choose Pattern, then use the Pattern pop-up palette to choose an available pattern.

You cannot use the Paint Bucket on images in Bitmap mode.

4 Deselect the Contiguous option to allow the Paint Bucket to colour pixels anywhere in the image, provided that they fall within the Tolerance setting.

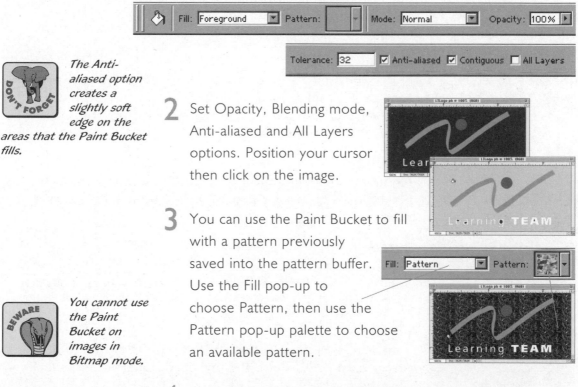

Blending Modes

The blending modes allow you to make changes to an image using the painting and editing tools in a more selective and subtle way than simply painting with the foreground colour. The colour you paint with (the blend colour) combines with the colour of the pixels you drag across (the base colour) to produce a different colour depending on the blending mode you select.

Choose blending modes from the pop-up menu in the Painting Tool Options palettes. The various paint modes in combination with opacity/pressure settings have a selective control on which pixels are affected when you use the painting and editing tools. The result is more of a blending of the paint colour and the colour of the base pixels than simply one colour replacing another.

Dissolve

Produces a grainy, chalk-like effect. Not all pixels are coloured as you drag across the image, leaving gaps and holes in the stroke. Use Opacity to control the effect.

Behind

Only available when you are working on a layer with a transparent background. Use Behind to paint behind the existing pixels on a layer. Paint appears in the transparent areas, but does not affect the existing pixels.

Multiply

Combines the colour you are painting with the colour of the pixels you drag across, to produce a colour that is darker than the original colours.

Screen

Produces the opposite effect to Multiply. It multiplies the opposite of the original colour by the painting colour and has the effect of lightening the pixels.

Overlay

This increases the contrast and saturation, combining foreground colour with the pixels you drag across.

Blending modes are also available in the Layers palette and in the Fill Path, Fill, Stroke and Fade dialogue boxes.

Soft Light

Creates a soft lighting effect. Lightens colours if the painting colour is lighter than 50% grey, darkens colours if the painting colour is darker than 50% grey.

Hard Light

Multiplies or screens pixels, depending on the paint colour, and tends to increase contrast.

Darken

Applies the paint colour to pixels that are lighter than the paint colour – doesn't change pixels darker than the paint colour.

Lighten

Replaces pixels darker than the paint colour, but does not change pixels lighter than the paint colour.

Difference

It looks at the brightness of pixels and the paint colour, then subtracts paint brightness from pixel brightness. Depending on the result, it inverts the pixels.

Exclusion

The result is similar to Difference, but with lower contrast.

Hue

In colour images, applies the hue (colour) of the paint, without affecting the saturation or luminosity of the base pixels.

Saturation

Changes the saturation of pixels based on the saturation of the blend colour, but does not affect hue or luminosity.

Luminosity

Changes the relative lightness or darkness of the pixels without affecting their hue or saturation.

Colour

Applies the hue and saturation of the blend colour, but does not affect the luminosity of the base pixels.

Colour Dodge

Lightens the base colour – more pronounced when the paint colour is light.

Colour Burn

Darkens the base colour – more pronounced when paint colour is dark.

Defining a Brush

You can create your own custom brush strokes from selections.

1 To create a brushstroke, make a selection, then choose Edit > Define Brush. The new brush is added to the Brushes palette.

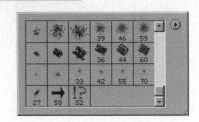

2 Click the brush size icon in the Options bar if you want to change the spacing and anti-aliased options. Anti-aliased is not available for very large brush sizes.

3 You can then use a painting tool to paint with the new brush. In this example a fade of 30 has been set.

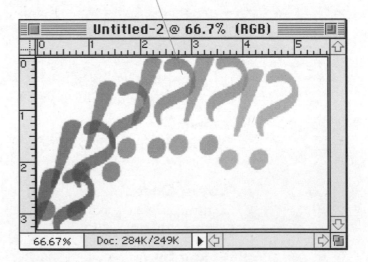

Creating Shape Layers

The shape tools allow you to create lines, rectangles and ovals and circles. In Photoshop you can also create Polygons and Custom shapes. Use the Options bar to set specific options for each tool individually.

The Polygon, Custom Shape, Pen and Freeform Pen tools are available in Photoshop only.

1 To draw a rectangle as a shape layer, first choose a foreground colour for the shape. Select the Rectangle tool. Make sure the Create New Shape Layer button is selected in the Options bar.

Change the colour of a shape layer by editing its fill layer. Change the outline of the shape by editing the layer clipping path using the Direct Selection tool.

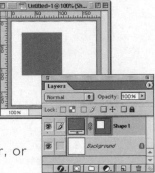

2 Position your cursor in the image window. Drag diagonally to define the size of the shape. A new shape layer appears in the Layers palette. To create additional shapes on the same shape layer, either choose a new shape tool from the Options bar, or use the same tool.

3 Click the OK button in the Options bar, or press Enter/Return to commit the changes to the shape layer and to deselect the drawing tools.

Use the pop-up triangle to the right of the Shape drawing tools in the Options bar to set specific options for tools if required.

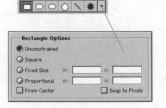

4 To draw a square, hold down Shift, then drag with the Rectangle tool. Release the mouse button before you release the Shift key, otherwise the constraint effect will be lost. Hold down Alt, then drag with the rectangle tool to draw a rectangle from the centre out.

5 Select the Shape layer icon (a highlight border appears around the Shape layer icon), then use the Direct Selection tool to make changes to the shape of the object on the Shape layer.

Creating Rasterised Shapes

A rasterised shape is a shape comprised of pixels. It is not based on a vector path and cannot be edited in the same way as a shape layer.

1 To create a rasterised shape, select a layer, or create a new layer. Select a foreground colour for the shape.

2 Select either the Rectangle, Rounded Rectangle, Ellipse, Line, Polygon or Custom Shape tool.

3 Select the Create Filled Region button in the Options bar.

You cannot create a rasterised shape on a vector based shape layer or a type layer.

4 Position your cursor in the image window. Drag diagonally to define the size of the shape. The shape appears in the window. It does not automatically create a new layer. A rasterised shape is the equivalent of creating a selection, then filling it with a colour.

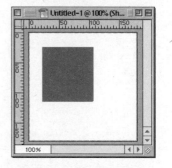

The Polygon tool and the Custom Shape tools are not available in ImageReady.

5 For the Polygon tool, you can set a number of sides for the shape in the Options bar. Click on the settings pop-up triangle to access further controls for creating polygons or stars.

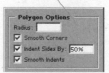

The Editing Tools

The editing tools – Blur and Sharpen, Smudge, Clone and Pattern Stamp, Dodge, Burn, Sponge and Eraser – allow you to edit or change pixels in a variety of ways.

The editing tools can be used within a selection or anywhere on an image. Use the Brushes palette to specify a brush size for the editing tool. Many of the techniques and keyboard shortcuts covered for the painting tools apply to the editing tools as well.

Covers

Chapter Seven

The Blur, Sharpen and Smudge Tools (R)

The Blur Tool

The Blur and Sharpen tools are the two 'Focus' tools. The Blur tool works by reducing contrast between pixels and can be useful for disguising unwanted, jagged edges and softening edges between shapes.

Remember to set an appropriate brush size before you start working with the Blur/ Sharpen tool.

1 To blur areas of your image, select the Blur tool. If the Blur Options bar is not showing, you can double-click the Blur tool to show it.

2 Set the Blend mode, Pressure and Use All Layers options, position your cursor on the image, then click and drag to blur the pixels. Release the mouse then drag across the pixels again to intensify the effect.

You cannot use the Blur/ Sharpen tool on an image in Bitmap or Indexed Colour mode.

The Sharpen Tool

The Sharpen tool works by increasing the contrast between pixels.

1 To sharpen areas of an image, select the Sharpen tool.

2 Position your cursor, then click and drag to sharpen the pixels. Click and drag across the same area of the image again, to intensify the sharpening effect. You will produce a coarse, grainy effect if you overuse the Sharpen tool. Use a low pressure setting and build up the effect gradually.

Each Focus tool retains its own settings when you switch to the other tool.

The Smudge Tool

You can use the Smudge tool to create an effect similar to dragging your finger through wet paint. The Smudge tool picks up colour from where you start to drag and smears it into adjacent colours.

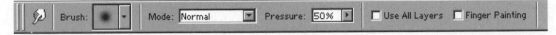

Hold down Alt to temporarily turn Finger Painting on or off, depending on whether the option is selected in the Options palette.

1 Select the Smudge tool. Set the Pressure, position your cursor on the image, then start to drag across your image to smudge the colours. The higher the pressure setting, the more pronounced the effect.

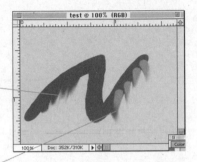

2 Select the Finger Painting option if you want to begin the smudge with the current foreground colour.

3 Select the Use All Layers option if you want to smudge colours from other layers in the image onto the layer you are working on. Leave this option deselected if you want the smudge to pick up colour from pixels on the active or target layer only.

Use All Layers

Select this option when you want Photoshop to take into account, or 'sample', pixels from layers other than the target layer. In other words, it samples from layers as if they were merged.

The Clone and Pattern Stamp Tools (S)

You can use the Clone Stamp tool to retouch an image by cloning or duplicating areas of it. This is very useful when you want to remove blemishes and scratches. Use the Pattern Stamp tool to paint with a predefined pattern.

The Clone Stamp Tool

1 To clone an area of your image, select the Clone Stamp tool. Remember to set an appropriate brush size using the Brushes pop-up palette in the Options bar.

2 Make sure that the Aligned option is selected. Hold down Alt and click on the part of the image you want to clone.

3 Release Alt. Move the cursor to a different image part, then click and drag. The pixels in the image where you drag are replaced by pixels cloned from the spot where you first clicked. A crosshair at the point where you first clicked indicates the pixels that are being cloned – the source point.

Clone – Aligned

With the Aligned option selected, the distance from the source point (shown by the crosshair) to the Clone Stamp cursor remains fixed. This means that you can release the mouse, move the cursor, then continue to use the Clone Stamp tool. The relative position of the source point and the Rubber Stamp cursor remains constant, but you will now be cloning pixels from a different part of the image.

Clone – Non-aligned

With the Aligned option off, the source point – where you first click – remains the same. If you stop dragging with the Clone Stamp cursor, move to a different part of the image, then start dragging again, the pixels you clone continue to come from the original source point.

The Pattern Stamp Tool

The Pattern Stamp tool works in a similar way to the Clone Stamp tool, but it paints with a predefined area of pixels – the pattern – rather than from a variable source point in the image.

1 To define a pattern, select an area to use as a pattern (using the Rectangular Marquee tool: – see page 98), then choose Edit > Define Pattern.

2 Choose the Pattern Stamp tool. Check your brush size, choose a pattern from the Pattern pop-up menu. Position your cursor on the image, then click and drag to paint with the pattern.

Pattern – Aligned

With the Aligned option selected, even if you stop dragging and then restart, the pattern aligns seamlessly.

Pattern – Non-aligned

This option paints with the predefined pattern, but does not align seamlessly if you stop dragging and then restart dragging.

The Dodge, Burn and Sponge Tools (O)

The Dodge, Burn, Saturate/Desaturate group of tools are collectively called the 'Toning' tools. The Dodge and Burn tools are based on the traditional photographic technique of decreasing the amount of exposure given to a specific area on a print to lighten it (dodging), or increasing the exposure to darken areas (burning-in).

The Dodge Tool

Use the Dodge tool to lighten pixels in your image.

You cannot use the Dodge, Burn or Saturate/ Desaturate tools on an image in Bitmap or Indexed Colour mode.

1 To lighten areas of an image, select the Dodge tool. Remember to choose an appropriate brush size. A soft-edged brush usually creates the smoothest result. If the Options bar is not showing, you can double-click the Dodge tool to show it.

2 Set the Range pop-up menu to Midtones, Shadows or Highlights to limit changes to the middle range of greys, the dark or light areas of the image respectively, and also set Exposure to control the intensity of the tool.

It's a good idea to use a low exposure setting when you lighten areas of an image and build up the effect gradually.

3 Position your cursor on the image, then click and drag to lighten the pixels. Release the mouse then drag across the pixels again to intensify the effect.

The Burn Tool

Use the Burn tool to darken pixels in your image.

1 To darken areas of an image, select the Burn tool.
Remember to choose an appropriate brush size.
A soft-edged brush usually creates the smoothest result.

2 Set the Range pop-up to Midtones, Shadows or Highlights to limit changes to the middle range of greys, the dark or light areas of the image respectively, and also set Exposure.

3 Position your cursor on the image, then click and drag to lighten the pixels. Release the mouse then drag across the pixels again to intensify the effect.

The Sponge Tool

In Greyscale Mode, the Sponge tool has the effect of increasing or decreasing contrast.

You can use the Sponge tool when you want to subtly increase or decrease colour saturation in areas of your image.

1 To saturate/desaturate areas of an image, select the Sponge tool. Remember to select an appropriate brush size.

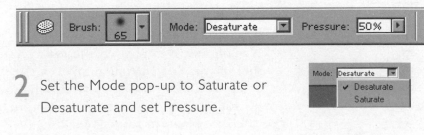

Each Toning tool retains its own settings when you switch to the other tools in the same group.

2 Set the Mode pop-up to Saturate or Desaturate and set Pressure.

3 Position your cursor on the image, then click and drag to alter the saturation.

The Eraser Tool (E)

Use the Eraser tool to erase portions of your image. The Eraser rubs out to the background colour when you are working on the Background layer. It erases to transparency when you are working on any other layer, provided that the Lock Transparent pixels option is not selected in the Layers palette.

Use the Brushes palette to specify the Eraser size when using the tool in Paintbrush, Pencil and Airbrush mode.

1 To erase areas of your image, select the Eraser tool (E) to show Eraser options in the Options bar. Use the bar to specify Mode, Opacity, Fade, Wet Edges and Erase to History options.

2 Click and drag on your image to erase to the background colour or transparency, depending on the layer on which you are working.

Opacity
Use the opacity setting to create the effect of partially erasing pixels.

Hold down Alt with the Eraser tool selected to access the Erase to History option temporarily. Click and drag across modified areas of the image to restore them to the specified state in the History palette.

Mode
Use the Erasing Mode pop-up to choose an erase mode. The default is Paintbrush. Block is useful when you need to erase along straight edges. The Block eraser is a fixed size square.

Erase to History
Use the Erase to History option to return pixels to their status at a particular state in the History palette. Click in the History Brush column in the History palette to set the state to which the Erase to History option returns pixels.

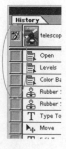

The Magic Eraser (E)

Use the Magic Eraser tool to erase pixels on a layer to transparency. The Magic Eraser works best when you want to remove the background pixels around a hard-edged object.

The Magic Eraser tool erases pixels based on a tolerance level, similar to the way in which the Magic Wand works. (See page 105 for information on the Magic Wand.)

The Magic Eraser tool is grouped with the Eraser tool. Press and hold on the Eraser tool to access the tools in the tool group. You can also use the keyboard shortcut Shift+E to cycle through the Eraser tools.

1 To use the Magic Eraser tool, first select the layer on which you want to work.

2 Select the Magic Eraser tool to show the Magic Eraser options in the Options bar.

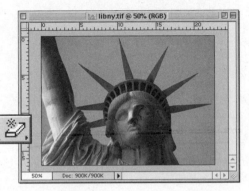

3 Enter a tolerance value. Set a low tolerance value to erase only those pixels that are very similar in colour value to the pixel on which you first click. Set a high tolerance value to select a wider range of pixels.

The Tolerance value extends or limits the number of pixels that are erased.

4 Set an Opacity value of 100% to erase pixels completely. Set a lower Opacity value to create a partially transparent effect.

5 Select the Use All Layers option to erase pixels based on a sample that takes into account colour values from all visible layers, not only the currently active layer.

6 Select the Anti-aliased option to create a smoother edge when pixels are erased. (See page 99 for further information on anti-aliasing).

7 Select the Contiguous option to erase only pixels that fall within the tolerance value specified, and that are adjacent to each other. This option erases continuous areas of pixels. Deselect the Contiguous option if you want the Magic Eraser to erase all pixels that fall within the tolerance value anywhere in the image.

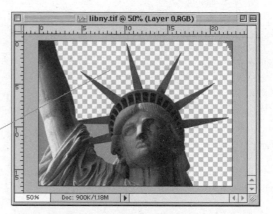

8 Position the cursor, then click to erase pixels that fall within the tolerance value.

The Background Eraser (E)

Use the Background Eraser tool when you are working on a layer to erase pixels to transparency. You can set tolerance and sampling values to control the level of transparency and the sharpness of its boundary edges.

The settings you choose have greatest effect at the hotspot. The strength of the effect diminishes further away from the hotspot.

The Background Eraser cursor displays a crosshair at the centre of the brush cursor. This indicates the tool's 'hotspot' – the point at which the tool's settings have greatest effect.

1 To erase pixels on a layer, select the Background Eraser tool. Select a layer on which you want to work.

2 Select the Background Eraser tool to show its options in the Options bar.

3 Choose Contiguous to remove adjacent pixels that fall within the tolerance setting. (Discontiguous erases pixels throughout the image, Find Edges preserves sharp edges along objects).

4 Set a Tolerance value (using the tolerance field), or drag the Tolerance slider. Set a low tolerance value to limit the effect to pixels that are very similar in colour value to pixels at the 'hotspot'. Set a high tolerance value to erase a broader range of similar colours.

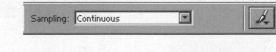

5 Choose a Sampling option. Select Continuous to erase all colours that you drag the Background Eraser tool across.

Select Once to erase pixels that are the same colour as the pixel on which you first click. This is useful when you want to erase areas of solid colour. Select Background Swatch only if you want to erase areas containing the currently set Background colour.

Be careful about the hotspot – keep it away from pixels in the layer that you don't want to erase. Modify your settings if you find that you are erasing pixels you don't want to erase.

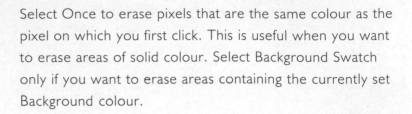

6 Select the Protect Foreground Colour if you want to prevent the tool from erasing any pixels that match the currently set Foreground colour.

7 Choose a Brush size from the Brushes palette.

Use the [or] keys on the keyboard to decrease/ increase the size of the Background Eraser brush as you work.

8 Position your cursor on a layer, then drag to erase pixels on the layer to transparency, based on the settings you have chosen.

Making Selections

One of the most important techniques when using Photoshop is making selections. When you make a selection, you are selecting an area of the image to which you want to make changes, and isolating the remainder of the image so that it is not affected by changes. A selection is indicated on-screen by a selection marquee – sometimes referred to as the 'marching ants' border.

Covers

Chapter Eight

The Marquee Selection Tool (M)

The Marquee selection tools allow you to drag with the mouse to make selections. You can make rectangular or elliptical selections by choosing the appropriate tool.

If you are working on an image with more than one layer, make sure you select the appropriate target layer before you make a selection.

1 To make a rectangular or oval selection, choose the Rectangular or Elliptical Marquee tool.

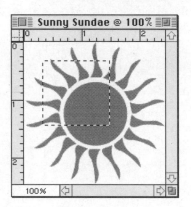

2 Position your cursor on the image, then click and drag to define the area you want to select. When you release the cursor you will see a dotted rectangular or oval marquee defining the area of the selection.

Hold down Shift, then click and drag with the Rectangular or Elliptical Marquee tool to create a square or circular selection. Hold down Alt to create a selection from the centre out.

3 You can reposition the selection marquee if you need to. Make sure the Marquee tool is still selected, position your cursor inside the selection marquee (the cursor changes shape), then click and drag. You can move selection marquees with any of the Selection tools.

4 With the Marquee tool selected, you can deselect a selection by clicking inside or outside the selection marquee. Alternatively, you can choose Select > Deselect (Command/ Ctrl+D).

As you are dragging to create a selection, you can hold down the Spacebar to reposition the marquee.

Marquee Options

You can use the Marquee Options palette to make changes to the way in which the Marquee tools work.

1 Select the Rectangular or Elliptical Marquee tool. Make sure the New Selection button is selected in the Options bar.

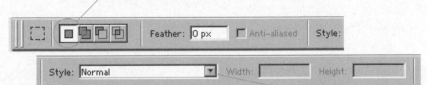

2 Use the Style pop-up to create settings for making proportional selections, or selections of a fixed size.

3 The Anti-aliased option is an important control when using bitmap applications such as Photoshop. Select anti-aliased to create a slightly blurred, soft edge around the selection and the pixels that surround the selection. Using Anti-aliased helps avoid creating unwanted jagged edges.

4 Use the Feather entry field to create a soft, feathered edge. (See pages 106–107 in this chapter.)

Moving Selections

You can use the Selection tools to reposition a selection border, but you must use the Move tool if you want to move pixels from one location to another.

I Make a selection. Select the Move tool (V) and then position your cursor inside the Marquee selection border. Click and drag to move the selection. Alternatively, with the Marquee, Lasso or Magic Wand tool still selected, hold down Command/Ctrl. The cursor changes temporarily to the Move tool cursor. Click and drag to move the selected pixels.

To move the selection in increments of one pixel with the Move tool selected, press the up, down, left or right arrow keys. Hold down Shift and press the arrow keys to move the selection in increments of five pixels.

When you move pixels on the Background layer, the area from which the pixels are moved is filled with the current background colour.

As long as the selection border remains selected, you can continue to move the pixels. Whilst the selection is active, the pixels in the selection 'float' above the underlying pixels, without replacing them.

2 To 'defloat' the pixels so that they replace the underlying pixels, choose Select > Deselect if you have the Move tool selected. If you used Command/Ctrl with a Marquee or Lasso tool selected, click outside the selection marquee. If you used Command/Ctrl with the Magic Wand tool selected, choose Select > Deselect. As soon as you deselect, the pixels on the Background layer that were underneath the floating selection – the underlying pixels – are now completely replaced by the pixels in the floating selection.

3 Notice that the area that the pixels in the selection were moved from is filled with the currently selected background colour. (In a bitmap image, you cannot have an area where there are no pixels.)

4 To move a selection and make a copy of it at the same time, hold down Alt before you drag with the Move tool. Alternatively, with a selection tool selected, hold down Command/Ctrl+Alt, then click and drag. The cursor turns into a double-headed arrow, indicating that you are copying the selection.

5 You can turn a 'floating' selection into a layer by choosing Layer > New > Layer Via Cut/Layer Via Copy (See Chapter 9 – Layers for further information.)

The Lasso Tools (L)

You can use the Lasso tool to make freeform selections by clicking and dragging. It is a useful tool for selecting irregular areas and for quickly adding to or subtracting from selections made with the Magic Wand tool.

1 Double-click the Lasso tool to show the Lasso Options bar if it is not showing. Set Feather and Anti-aliased options.

Hold down Shift, then click and drag around an area to add it to the selection. Hold down Alt, then click and drag around an area to remove it from the selection.

2 Position your cursor on the image. The cursor changes to the Lasso cursor. Click and drag around the part of the image you want to select. Make sure your cursor comes back to the start point. If you release

before reaching the start point, Photoshop completes the selection with a straight line. A dotted marquee defines the selected area.

Polygon Lasso

Use the Polygon Lasso tool to create a freeform selection with straight line segments.

If you have a feather amount set in the Lasso Options palette, you will not end up with sharp corners on the selection.

1 Select the Polygon Lasso tool. Position your cursor on the image, then click; move the cursor, then click… and so on, until you have defined the area you want to select.

2 Click back at the start point to complete the selection. A small circle appears at the bottom right of the cursor to indicate the start. Alternatively, you can double-click to close the selection marquee.

The Magnetic Lasso

The Magnetic Lasso Tool is most useful when you want to select an object or an area of the image which contrasts strongly with the area surrounding it.

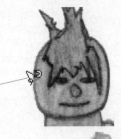

1 Press and hold on the Lasso tool, to select the Magnetic Lasso tool from the tool group. Click on the edge of the object you want to select to place the first fastening point.

A fastening point anchors the Selection Border in place as you create the selection. Fastening Points disappear when you close the selection border. The Magnetic Lasso adds fastening points at intervals to the selection border to anchor the segments.

2 Either, move the cursor along the edge of the object, or click and drag along the edge to draw a freehand segment. As you move along the edge of the object, the 'active' segment of the selection border snaps to the most clearly defined edge in the image (in the close proximity of the cursor). Fastening points are added automatically, at intervals, as you drag.

3 Click on the edge of the shape if you need to add a fastening point manually. Continue moving the cursor, or dragging and clicking, to continue making the selection border.

4 To close the selection border, position your cursor on the start point, (a small circle at the cursor indicates that you are on the start point) then click. Alternatively, double-click, or press the Enter/Return key. Photoshop will create a segment from the point you have reached to the start point of the selection border. To close the selection border with a straight line segment, hold down Alt and double-click.

Magnetic Lasso Options

As with all the tools you use in Photoshop, after you have clicked on the tool to select it, but before you start to use it, check the setting for the tool in the appropriate tool options palette.

Lasso Width

Enter a value between 1–40 to specify a detection width. The Magnetic Lasso tool detects edges only within the specified distance from the pointer.

Double-click the Magnetic Lasso tool to show the Magnetic Lasso Options bar if it is not already showing. (Or use Window > Show Options.)

Frequency

This setting determines the rate at which Fastening points are set. Enter a value between 0–100. The higher the value you set, the more frequently fastening points are placed.

Edge Contrast

Enter a value between 1–100%. This value determines how sensitive the Magnetic Lasso tool is to edges in the image. Higher values select edges that contrast strongly with their background. Lower values select edges that have smaller amounts of contrast.

If the object you are trying to select has high contrast (i.e., well defined edges) use higher Lasso Width and Edge Contrast settings. For objects with less well defined edges, use lower Lasso Width and Edge Contrast settings.

The Magic Wand Tool (W)

The Magic Wand tool selects continuous areas of colour in an image, based on a tolerance setting. Low tolerance settings create a very limited selection of colour. Higher settings select a wider range of pixels. The tool is good for selecting consistently coloured areas.

To add to a selection using the Magic Wand tool, hold down Shift, then click on an unselected part of the image.

| Before creating a selection using the Magic Wand tool, check the tolerance setting. Double-click the Magic Wand tool to display the Magic Wand Options bar if it is not showing, or choose Window > Show Options to show the Options bar. Enter a tolerance value from 0–255. If you set a tolerance value of 255, you will select every pixel in the image.

Tolerance: 32 ☑ Anti-aliased ☑ Contiguous ☐ Use All Layers

Typically, you will fine-tune Magic Wand selections using a combination of the other selection tools, together with the Grow and Similar commands.

2 Click on the image to select pixels of similar colour value. All adjacent pixels that are within the tolerance range are selected. Adjust the default setting of 32 as necessary to make the selection you require.

3 Deselect the Contiguous option to select pixels throughout the image that fall within the Tolerance setting. The result is similar to using the Similar command (see page 109).

You cannot use the Magic Wand tool in Bitmap mode.

4 To deselect a selection marquee when the Magic Wand tool is selected, click inside the selection marquee. If you click outside the selection marquee, you will create another selection based around the pixel where you clicked.

Feathering Selections

You can use the Feather option to control the degree to which the edge of a selection is softened or faded. Feathering a selection creates a transition boundary between the selection and the surrounding pixels, which can cause a loss of detail.

1 Select one of the Lasso tools, or the Elliptical Marquee selection tool. The Options bar updates according to the tool you select.

2 In the Options bar, set a feather value, e.g. 10. You can set a value from 1 to 250 pixels. The amount you set depends on the effect you want to achieve.

3 Create a selection using either the Marquee or Lasso tool. When you move the selection you will see the feathered edge around the selection and also where you move the selection from.

4 Alternatively, using any of the selection tools, you can make a selection and then choose Select > Feather. Enter a value for the Feather radius.

Creating a Vignette

You can use the feathering option to create a vignette effect – a soft, fading edge to an image.

1   Before you begin, make sure your background colour is set to white (see Chapter Five – Defining Colours). Then set a feather value in the Options bar for the selection tool you are using.

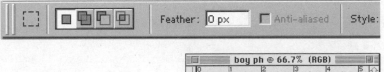

2   Next, create a selection, which can be a regular or irregular shape.

3   Choose Select > Inverse. This reverses the selection – selecting all the pixels that were previously not selected.

 Feathering, unlike anti-aliasing, blurs the inside and outside of a selection boundary.

4   Press Delete (Mac) or Backspace (Windows) to delete the area surrounding your selection, leaving a feathered edge.

Modifying Selections

Select a Selection tool, then click the Add to ... , Subtract from ... or Intersect with Selection button in the Options bar to modify an existing selection.

Beware, these settings remain in effect for the tool. It's worth reselecting the New Selection button, so that unwanted settings do not cause unexpected results the next time you use the tool.

For complex selections, it can be quite useful to hide the dotted selection border temporarily, in order to see the selected pixels more clearly. Choose View > Show > Selection Edges to hide the selection border. The selection remains active; you have simply hidden the border. Choose the same option to redisplay the selection border.

Alternatively, choose View > Show Extras (Command/ Ctrl+H) to hide/show selection edges and any guides, grids, slices or paths.

There are many instances when you need to add to or subtract from a selection. You can use any combination of selection tools to make the selection you want. For example, you might start by making a selection with the Magic Wand tool, then add to the selection using the Lasso tool.

1   To add to an existing selection, hold down the Shift key, then click and drag to create another selection marquee that intersects the existing selection marquee.

2   You can use the same technique to create non-adjoining selections. Although the selections may be in different parts of the image, they count and act as one selection. For example, if you apply a filter, the effect will be apparent in all the selection marquees.

3   To add to a selection, hold down Shift and use the Lasso tool to quickly loop around small areas that the Magic Wand tool typically misses out from its selection.

4   To subtract from a selection, hold down Alt, then click and drag with a selection tool to intersect the existing selection marquee. The area defined by the intersecting marquee will be removed from the original selection.

The Grow and Similar Commands

The Grow and Similar commands are very useful when used in conjunction with the Magic Wand tool to add to a selection. Both work according to the tolerance setting set in the Magic Wand Options palette.

The Grow command selects contiguous or adjoining areas of colour based on the tolerance setting in the Magic Wand Options palette.

If necessary, change the tolerance setting for the Magic Wand tool before using the Grow command to achieve a more, or less inclusive result.

1 Make a selection. Check that the Tolerance setting in the Magic Wand Options palette is appropriate.

2 Choose Select > Grow. Pixels which fall within the Tolerance setting and are adjacent to pixels already in the selection are added to the selection.

The Similar command selects non-adjacent pixels that fall within the same tolerance setting as set in the Magic Wand Options palette.

Using the Magic Wand tool, with the Contiguous option (in the Options bar) deselected, is the equivalent of using the Similar command.

1 Make a selection using any of the selection tools. Check that the Tolerance setting in the Magic Wand Options palette is appropriate.

2 Choose Select > Similar. Pixels throughout the image that fall within the Tolerance setting are selected.

Pasting Into Selections

Pasting into selections is a useful technique for compositing images.

When you paste into a selection, the selection from the clipboard will be rendered at the resolution of the destination document. This means that the selection from the source document will change size if the resolution of the two documents is different.

1 Create a selection in the destination window.

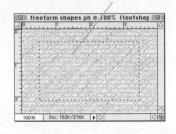
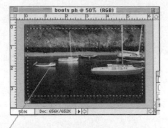

2 Open the source document, then make the selection you want to paste into the destination document. Choose Edit > Copy to copy the selection to the clipboard.

3 Click in the destination image window. The selection should still be active. Choose Edit > Paste Into (Command/Ctrl+Shift+V) to paste the clipboard selection into the selected area.

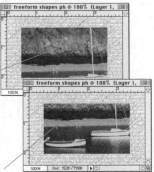

Make sure the layer mask is selected, then paint with black to add to the mask, or paint with white to subtract from the mask. (See pages 164–165, 'Layer Masks'.)

4 Use the Move tool to reposition the pasted selection relative to the original selection.

5 The Paste Into command creates a layer mask. The layer is active, indicated by the paintbrush icon in the Layers palette, which means that you can edit the layer. To edit the mask, click the mask icon in the Layers palette. A small circle replaces the paintbrush, indicating that the layer mask is selected.

The Defringe Command

You can drag a selection from one window to another image window. This is useful when creating a composite image. Defringe is useful when you use this technique, as it helps to blend the selection into its new environment.

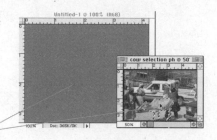

1 To drag a selection from one image window to another, first make a selection in the source window. Select the Move tool, position the Move cursor inside the selection, then click and drag into the destination window.

2 When you release the mouse button, the selection appears in the destination window on a new layer. The destination window becomes the active window, and the new layer is the active layer. Check to see if there are unwanted pixels causing a halo effect around the edge of the selection.

3 To defringe the moved selection, make sure the newly created layer is active. Choose Layer > Matting > Defringe. Enter a value for the width, then OK the dialogue box. The selection should now blend in better.

Filling a Selection

You can use the Fill dialogue box to fill an entire layer or a selection.

To fill a selection, first define either a foreground or background colour that you want to fill with, then make a selection. Choose Edit > Fill. Use the Contents pop-up to choose the fill type. You can also set Opacity for the fill and a Blending Mode. OK the dialogue box.

See pages 80–81 for a description of the blending modes.

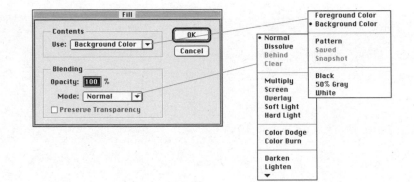

To fill a selection with a pattern, first define the pattern by making a selection, then choosing Edit > Define Pattern.

Make the selection you want to fill with the previously defined pattern.

Choose Edit > Fill. Choose Pattern from the Contents pop-up. Use the Custom Pattern pop-up menu to choose the pattern. OK the dialogue box to fill the selection with the pattern.

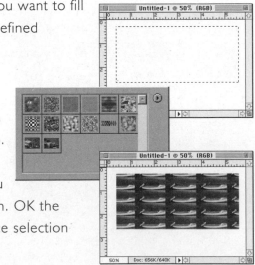

Copying and Pasting Selections

You can use the clipboard to copy and past selections within the same image and into other images.

A useful technique for selecting a simple image, like the runner on this page, is the Inverse selection command. Use the Magic Wand tool to select the background, then choose Select > Inverse to reverse the selection. The areas that represent the runner are now selected.

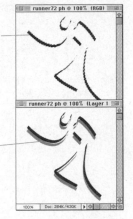

1 To copy a selection, first make a selection using any of the selection tools. Choose Edit > Copy.

2 To paste the selection into the same image, choose Edit > Paste. The selection is pasted into the image on its own layer. (For information on working with layers, see Chapter Nine, 'Layers'.)

3 To paste the selection into another image, click on the other image window if it is already open, or use File > Open to open another image. Choose Edit > Paste to paste the selection from the clipboard onto a new layer in the active image.

4 You can also drag a selection from one image window into another. You need two images open – the source and the destination windows. Make a selection in the source window, select the Move tool, position your cursor within the selection, then click and drag into the destination window. The selection appears on its own layer.

Use the Defringe command (see page 111) to help a pasted or dragged selection blend into its new surroundings.

Transforming Selections

The ability to transform a selection's bounding box enables you to fine tune selections, distort selections and make selections that were previously difficult to achieve.

1 To transform a selection, choose Select > Transform Selection. A bounding box with eight handles appears around the selection. A Point of Origin marker appears at the centre of the bounding box.

2 To scale a selection, click and drag a handle. The cursor becomes a bidirectional arrow ( ). To scale a selection in proportion, hold down Shift then drag a handle.

3 To rotate a selection, position your cursor just outside the selection border. The cursor changes to a bi-directional, curved arrow ( ). Click and drag in a circular direction.

4 To distort the selection boundary, hold down Command/Ctrl then drag a corner handle.

5 To create a perspective effect on the selection border, hold down Command/Ctrl+Alt+Shift, then drag a corner handle.

6 To shear a selection border, hold down Command/Ctrl, then click and drag a centre top/bottom or centre left/right handle.

7 Press the Esc key to remove the transform bounding box without applying any of the changes. Press return/Enter, or double-click inside the bounding box to accept the transformation.

Layers

Layers introduce a considerable degree of flexibility into the way in which you can work. Layers let you keep various image elements separate so that you can make changes without deleting or changing the underlying pixels.

Each additional layer you create increases the file size of the image. You can selectively merge layers into each other to help manage and consolidate layers as you work. When you have finished editing your image, you can flatten the image to merge all layers into a single background layer. You will need to do this to use your image in QuarkXPress or Adobe PageMaker. You should note that you can only save images with layers in Photoshop format.

Covers

Chapter Nine

Working with Layers

When you create or open an image for the first time, it consists of one default layer called Background.

New layers are automatically created when you use the Type tool to add text to an image, when you drag or copy a selection into an image, and also when you drag a layer from one document into another.

To edit Layer Options for a Layer, double-click the layer name. The Layer Options dialogue box appears. Make changes as necessary, then OK the dialogue box.

One of the most useful techniques for creating a new layer is to make a selection on a part of the background layer, then choose Layer > New > Layer via Copy (Command/Ctrl+J). The selection of pixels is copied to a new layer. You can now edit and transform the pixels on the new layer with the original pixels intact on the background layer.

To access the Layers palette, choose Window > Show Layers.

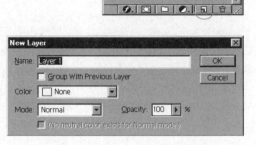

1 To create a new layer, either click once on the New Layer icon at the bottom of the Layers palette, or use the pop-up menu in the Layers palette and choose New Layer.

2 Enter a name for the layer in the New Layer dialogue box. You can also choose Opacity and Blending Mode settings at this stage if you want to.

3 OK the dialogue box, or press Return/Enter. The new layer appears in the Layers palette above the previously highlighted layer. Notice also that the file size in the Document Sizes status bar area increases when you paint on the layer or add pixels to the layer.

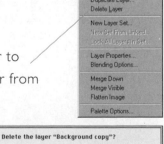

4 To delete a layer, click on the layer to select it. Then choose Delete Layer from the pop-up menu in the Layers palette. Click Yes or No in the Delete Layer warning box. Alternatively, drag the Layer name onto the Wastebasket icon at the bottom of the Layers palette.

Selecting, Hiding and Showing Layers

You can only work on one layer at a time. This is often referred to as the 'target' or active layer.

You can also click the eye icon to hide/show a layer set and a layer style.

1 Click on the layer name in the Layers palette to make it active. The layer name will highlight and the Paintbrush icon will appear in the second column on the left of the palette. The name of the active layer appears in the title bar of the image window.

To select all pixels on a layer, hold down Command/Ctrl and click on the layer name in the Layers palette.

2 To hide a layer, click on the eye icon in the leftmost column of the Layers palette. To show a layer, click in the leftmost column to bring back the eye icon.

Reordering Layers

It is often necessary to reorder the stacking position of layers to control which layers appear in front of other layers.

You can move pixels in a layer beyond the edge of your picture. These non-visible pixels will be saved with the document. Non-visible pixels are lost when you flatten the image.

1 To change the layering order, click and drag the layer name you want to reposition. Notice the black horizontal bar that appears as you move the layer upwards or downwards. Release the mouse when the black bar appears in the position to which you want the layer moved.

Layer 2
clock1.eps
Sunny Sundae eps
Layer 1
Background

Repositioning Layers

You can reposition the entire contents of a layer using the Move tool.

You can nudge the contents of a selected layer in 1-pixel increments by pressing the arrow keys when the Move tool is selected.

1 Click on the layer you want to move in the Layers palette. Select the Move tool, then position your cursor anywhere on the image. Click and drag to move the layer.

Merging and Flattening Layers

Use the Merge commands to combine two or more layers into one layer. This is useful for keeping file size down and for consolidating elements on different layers into a single manageable layer or unit.

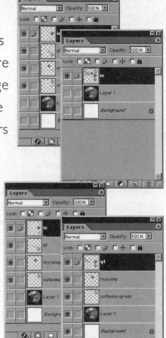

1 To merge all the visible layers in your document, first hide any layers you don't want to merge, make sure one of the layers you want to merge is active, then choose Merge Visible from the pop-up menu in the Layers palette, or choose Layer > Merge Visible.

2 To merge a layer with the layer below it, first select the layer, then choose Merge Down from the pop-up menu, or choose Layer > Merge Down.

Flattening Images

When you flatten an image, you end up with a Background layer only. This reduces the file size. Flatten an image when you have finished creating and positioning the elements of your composite image, and are ready to save the file in a suitable format for placing in a page layout application.

1 To flatten an image, make sure that all the layers you want to keep are visible. Choose Flatten Image from the Layers palette pop-up menu, or choose Layers > Flatten Image.

Moving Layers Between Images

The layer you move into the destination image window is rendered at the resolution of the destination window. This may cause the elements on the moved layer to appear larger or smaller than in the original window. To avoid surprises, make sure that the source and destination images are at the same resolution.

Also, if the modes of the two images are different, the layer you move will be converted to match the mode of the destination window.

You can copy a complete layer from one Photoshop document to another, similar to the way you move a selection from one document to another.

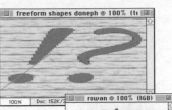

1 First make sure you have two document windows open – a 'source' document and a 'destination' document. The source document contains the layer you want to copy. The destination document is the document into which you want to copy the layer.

2 Click in the source document window to make it active. Position your cursor on the layer in the Layers palette, then drag the layer you want to copy from the source document into the destination document window. You will see a bounding box indicating the layer you are copying.

Use the Defringe command (see page 111) to remove any fringe around pixels on a layer that you copy from one image to another.

3 Position the layer and then release the mouse. The layer is positioned above the previously active layer in the Layers palette of the destination document. The destination document is now the active image window.

Linking Layers

Linking layers is useful when you want to keep elements of an image on separate layers, but you need to move the layers maintaining the exact positional relationship of each.

The principle of linking layers works, even if the layers are not next to each other in the Layers palette.

1 To move the foreground object with its shadow (which is on a separate layer), show the Layers palette (Window > Show Layers) and make sure that one of the layers you want to link is active.

2 Click in the empty box to the right of the eye icon of the layer you want to link. A chain icon appears in the box, indicating that the layer is linked. When you make the linked layer active, the chain and paintbrush icons switch to indicate the layer you are working on.

3 Use the Move tool to reposition the elements on the linked layers as one.

4 You can link multiple layers using the same technique.

5 To unlink a layer, click the chain icon. The layer is now completely independent again.

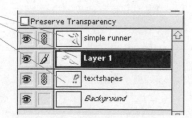

Adjustment Layers

An adjustment layer is created above the currently active layer. Its settings are applied to the layers below it and do not affect layers above.

Using an adjustment layer is like positioning a lens above the pixels on the layers below it to change their appearance. If you don't like the result, you can edit the adjustment layer to achieve the result you want, or you can discard the adjustment layer. When you are satisfied with the result you can implement the adjustment layer as a permanent change.

1 Select a layer in the Layers palette. The adjustment layer will be positioned above the currently active layer. Choose Layer > New Adjustment Layer.

2 Choose a type from the New Adjustment Layer sub-menu. This automatically becomes the name for the layer. Enter a different name if desired. Set Opacity and Blending Mode at this stage if you want to. Click OK.

You can restack adjustment layers as any other layer.

3 Depending on the type of adjustment layer you chose, the appropriate dialogue box opens. Create the settings you want to experiment with. OK the dialogue box.

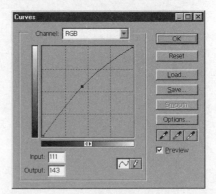

4 The new adjustment layer appears in the Layers palette as the active layer. The settings you created are now applied to all layers below the adjustment layer.

5 Click the eye icon to hide/show the preview of the changes brought about by the adjustment layer settings. Double-click the adjustment layer to re-enter the appropriate adjustment dialogue box to make changes to the settings.

 The adjustment layer settings do not have a permanent effect on pixels until the layer is merged with other layers, or the image is flattened.

6 Drag the adjustment layer into the wastebasket if you want to discard the settings.

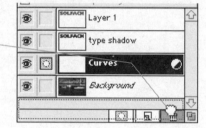

7 When you are ready to make the settings of the adjustment layer permanent, either use one of the Merge commands from the pop-up, or flatten the image.

Locking Layers

The background layer is automatically fully locked by default.

Transparent areas on a layer are indicated by the checkerboard pattern when the Background layer is hidden.

You can move locked layers to a new position in the stacking order of layers, but you cannot delete a locked layer.

Select a linked layer, then select the full lock option to lock all properties for the linked layers.

The Transparency lock and Image lock options are automatically selected for Type layers you create. You cannot turn these options off.

There are four levels of lock that can be applied to layers. A dimmed lock icon appears to the right of the layer when you select one of the lock options. A solid lock icon appears when the layer is fully locked.

1 To completely lock a layer, select the layer in the Layers palette, then click the full lock option. You will not be able to reposition the layer or make any changes to it, including changing blending mode, opacity and layer style.

2 To prevent the layer from being moved using the Move tool, click the Position lock option.

3 To disable painting tools on the layer, select the Image lock option. You can still edit any mask applied to the layer. You cannot move the layer. Selecting the Image lock option automatically locks transparency for the layer.

4 Click the Transparency lock to preserve

transparent areas of a layer. You can make changes to the existing pixels on the layer, but you cannot make changes to any areas of transparency. For example, if the Transparency lock is selected, the blur filters do not work on the layers as blurred pixels cannot be spread into the areas of transparency.

Layer Sets

When you create complex images with multiple layers it is convenient to simplify the layers palette by grouping related layers together into a Layer Set. Creating Layer Sets in complex, multi- layered images makes it much easier to manage the elements in the image.

1 To create a new layer set, click the New Layer Set button in the bottom of the Layers palette, or choose New Layer Set from the pop-up menu in the palette.

2 To create a layer set from existing layers, first link the layers you want to combine into a layer set. Choose New Set From Linked in the palette pop-up menu, or choose Layer > New > Layer Set from Linked.

To hide/reveal any layer styles applied to layers in a layer set, hold down Alt, then click the collapse/expand triangle.

3 To move a layer into a layer set, drag a layer onto the Layer Set folder. Release the mouse when the layer set folder highlights. The layer is positioned at the bottom of the layers already in the layer set. If the layer set is expanded, drag the layer to the desired position. Release when the highlight bar is in the correct position.

4 Click the collapse/expand triangle to reveal or hide the layers contained within the layer set.

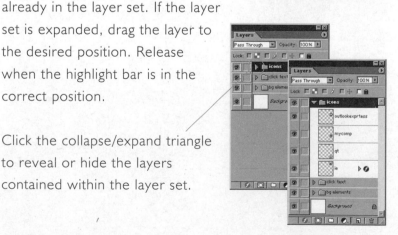

Layer Styles

Using the Layer Style sub-menu, you can create sophisticated layer effects such as soft shadows, bevelled and embossed edges, and inner and outer glows quickly and easily. This example consists of 3 layers – a White background layer, a coloured circle on its own layer and a coloured triangle on another layer, and uses Bevel and Emboss options to demonstrate the principles for creating a layer style.

Each layer style provides a range of options specific to that style. Experiment with the options to achieve the effect you want.

1 To apply a Layer Style, click on a layer in the Layers palette to make it active. Choose Layer > Layer Style > Bevel & Emboss. In the

Layer Style dialogue box, make sure the Preview option is selected to see the effect applied in the image.

You cannot apply a layer style to the background layer, a layer set or a locked layer.

2 In the Bevel and Emboss section, choose a style from the Style pop-up menu and a technique from the Technique pop-up menu. Select the Up/Down radio button to light the effect from above or below.

3 Use the Depth entry box or slider to adjust the height of the effect. Use the Size slider to control the amount of blur and the spread of the shadow. The Soften slider controls the overall intensity of the effect and helps reduce irregularities or artifacts in the shading.

4   In the Shading area, enter a value in the Angle entry box to control the direction of the light source. Enter a value in the Altitude entry box to define the apparent depth of the light source. Use the Angle/Altitude disk to create settings manually if you prefer.

5   Gloss Contours allow you to change the transition of the effect across the affected pixels on the layer.

6   Adjust settings for the Highlight and Shadow edges of the effect. It is a good idea initially to leave the blending modes set to Screen and Multiply respectively. Experiment with the Opacity sliders to create a more subtle effect.

7   OK the dialogue when you are satisfied with the results. Notice in the Layers palette an 'f' symbol (🄵) on the layer, indicating that there is a layer effect applied to the layer. Whilst the 'f' symbol appears the layer effect remains editable.

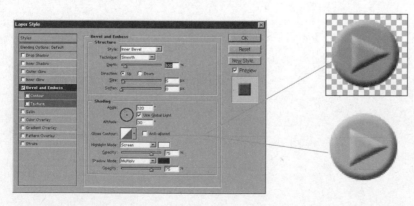

Managing Layer Styles

Once you have created a layer effect you can continue to edit the effect and you can use a variety of commands from the Layer Effects sub-menu to manage the effects.

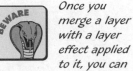

Once you merge a layer with a layer effect applied to it, you can no longer adjust the layer effect settings.

1 To edit the settings used to create a layer effect, make sure the appropriate layer is active, then click the expand triangle to display layer effects as separate entries in the Layers palette. Double-click the 'f' icon next to the name of the effect. You can continue to adjust settings as long as the layer displays the layer effects icon.

2 To temporarily disable layer effects on all layers, not just the active layer, choose Layer > Layer Style > Hide All Effects. Repeat the process to show all layer effects.

Choose Layer > Layer Style > Hide/Show All Layer Styles to display/hide all layer styles currently visible in the image.

3 To keep the angle of the light source constant if you are using multiple layer effects such as Drop Shadow, Bevel and Emboss and Satin, choose Layer > Layer Style > Global Light. Enter a value for the Angle in the Global Angle entry box. OK the dialogue box. Make sure you select the Use Global Light option when you create multiple layer effects in the Layer Style dialogue box.

4 To copy exact layer effect settings from one layer to another, first select a layer with a layer effect applied to it, then choose Copy Layer Style from the Layer Style sub-menu. Click on another layer in the Layers palette. Choose Paste Layer Style from the Layer Style sub-menu.

5 To permanently remove layer styles from a layer, make sure you select the appropriate layer, then choose Layer > Layer Style > Clear Layer Styles.

6 Layer Styles automate procedures that in the past you had to perform yourself. Use the Create Layer command from the Layer Styles sub-menu to separate the layer effect into the multiple layers that Photoshop has used to create the effect. This can be useful if you need to edit specific parts of the effect.

Transforming Layers

You cannot transform the Background layer in an image.

An advantage of using Free Transform is that you can make multiple transformations, then either accept or discard the result.

To use Perspective and Distort transformations on a type layer, you must first render (convert to pixels) the type layer – Layer > Type > Render Layer.

Position your cursor inside the bounding box, then click and drag, to reposition the layer whilst the transformation bounding box is still active.

The Transform sub-menu (Edit > Transform) gives alternative options for transforming layers.

Once you have moved pixels to a new layer you can then transform the layer. Using Free Transform you can scale, rotate, distort, skew and create perspective effects.

1 Ensure the layer is active. Choose Edit > Free Transform. A bounding box with handles appears around the pixels. To scale a layer, drag a handle. To scale in proportion, hold down Shift then drag a corner handle.

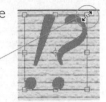

2 To rotate a layer, position your cursor slightly outside the bounding box. The cursor changes to a bi-directional arrow. Drag in a circular direction. You can drag the point of origin marker to a new position to specify the point around which the rotation takes place.

3 To skew the layer, hold down Command/ Ctrl+Shift, then drag the centre top/ bottom, or the centre left/right handle.

4 To create perspective, hold down Command/Ctrl+Alt+Shift then drag a corner handle. To distort the layer, hold down Command/Ctrl then drag a corner handle. This allows you to move corner handles independently.

5 To accept the transformation and remove the Transformation bounding box, press Return/Enter, or double-click inside the bounding box. To revert to the original state without making changes, press the Esc key.

The Extract Command

Use the Extract command to isolate an object from its background; especially useful when the object has edges that are not clearly or distinctly defined, such as hair.

Make sure you are working on a layer to use the Extract command. If you perform the Extract command on the Background layer it becomes Layer 0 when you OK the dialogue box.

There are 4 steps to extracting an object from its background. First, highlight the edges of the object. Second, define the interior of the object. Third, preview the results of the extraction. Four, depending on the preview, fine tune the extraction, then OK the dialogue box.

When the object and its background are similar in colour or have textures, select the Smart Highlight option. This creates a clearly defined edge, just wide enough to cover the edge, and is not dependent on the brush size.

Take your time, don't be tempted to rush the process of creating the highlighted edge.

Use the [or] keys to decrease/ increase the brush size in single increments.

1 To extract an object from its background, choose Image > Extract. Select the Edge Highlighter tool (B).

2 In the Tool Options area, set a brush size and choose a colour for the highlight edge from the Highlight pop-up.

3 Zoom in on the image if necessary, then draw around the object you want to extract to define the edge. It is important to create a highlight that slightly overlaps both the edge of the foreground object and its background. Use a larger brush size to completely cover more delicate, intricate, 'wispy' areas of the foreground object, such as hair; use a smaller brush size to highlight sharper, more defined edges.

Use Alt+Backspace to erase the entire highlight.

4 Use the Eraser tool to undo any mistakes you make with the Edge Highlighter tool. You cannot use the Undo command within the Extract dialogue box.

To use an alpha channel as the basis for a selection, choose the alpha channel from the Channel pop-up menu.

5 Make sure you completely enclose the object if it has a well-defined interior. It is not necessary to highlight edges where the object touches the edge of the image window.

6 Select the Fill tool (K). Click inside the highlight edge. The interior fills with the Fill colour set in the Tool Options area of the dialogue.

Use the Zoom and Hand tools as you would in the Photoshop image window. (See page 26 for further information).

7 Click the Preview button to preview the results. Use the Show pop-up in the Preview area to set the background against which you see the extracted object. It can help to preview against more than one background colour to pick up on any problem areas, before you click OK. (See page 133 for techniques to refine the extraction area.)

When you have filled an interior area with the Fill tool, clicking again in the fill area clears the fill.

8 Use the View pop-up to switch between the original and extracted images. Again, this is useful for making decisions about the results of the extraction before you OK the dialogue box.

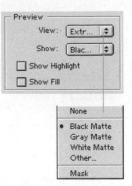

9 OK the dialogue box to complete the extraction.

Fine Tuning Extractions

After you preview the results of the extraction, you will need to fine tune it, before you OK the dialogue box.

 Use the Clean up tool to remove any unwanted pixels around the extraction after you preview it. Hold down Alt, then drag with the Clean up tool to refill any unwanted gaps in the extracted object.

 Use the Edge Touch up tool to create a more clearly defined, sharper edge in areas where there are problems with the extraction.

 Use the Smooth control in the Extraction area, if necessary, to improve the result of the extraction. The Smooth control can help remove stray artifacts from the extraction by feathering edges slightly.

1 To make adjustments to the extraction, select the Show Highlight option in the Preview area. The original highlight edge reappears.

2 Click the Show Fill option to show the original fill area for the extraction.

3 Choose Original from the View pop-up. The solid background against which you preview the results of the extraction disappears and the original background pixels reappear.

4 Select the Fill tool, then click inside the Fill area. This removes the fill highlight. Use the Eraser tool to erase parts of the highlight edge and use the Edge Highlighter tool to redefine areas of the edge, as necessary.

5 When you have finished editing the highlight edge, select the Fill tool, then click inside the edge to recreate the fill area. Click the Preview button to preview your changes. Repeat the editing process as necessary until you are satisfied with the result, then click OK.

New Layer Commands

The New Layer Via Cut (Command/Ctrl+Shift+J) and the New Layer Via Copy (Command/Ctrl+J) commands are essential options when creating layers. Use these commands to either cut or copy selected pixels to a new layer.

1 Start by making a selection. Then chose Layer > New > Layer Via Copy to create a new layer containing a copy of the selected pixels. The new layer is automatically named Layer 1, etc., depending on the number of layers already in the document.

2 Make a selection, then choose New Layer Via Cut to cut the selected pixels to a new layer. Notice when you reposition the pixels on the new layer, the area on the Background layer from which they were cut is filled with the current background colour.

Working with Type

You can now create and edit type directly in the image window. The type you create is preserved as vector outlines or paths which means that Photoshop can output type with sharp, resolution-independent edges.

The Masked Type option allows you to create complex selections in the shape of type characters.

You can choose different alignments vertically and horizontally for type, you can rotate it, fill it with a gradient, pattern or image, create translucent type and much more.

Covers

Chapter Ten

Creating Point Type

You can create two kinds of type: Point type and Paragraph type. Typically, you use Point type when you want to work with small amounts of text, such as a single character, word, or line. Use Paragraph type when you are working with more extensive blocks of type in paragraphs.

The small bar running through the bottom of the I-beam cursor indicates the position of the type's baseline.

1 To create Point type, select the Type tool (T). You can create settings for the type using options in the Options bar, or the Character and Paragraph palettes before you enter the type, or you can format the type after you enter it.

You can also commit type by pressing the Enter key on the numeric keypad, or choosing any other tool in the Toolbox.

2 Position your cursor in the image window, then click to place the text insertion point. Clicking with the Type tool takes Photoshop into Text Editing mode.

web

You must be in Text Editing mode to enter, edit or format text.

3 Enter text using the keyboard. You must press Enter (Windows), Return (Mac) on the main keyboard to begin a new line. Point type does not wrap.

4 Click on the Commit/OK button in the Options bar when you have finished entering or editing type to commit the type layer. This takes Photoshop out of Text Editing mode and you can now perform other tasks on the image. The type appears on its own layer.

For images in Multichannel, Bitmap or Indexed colour mode, type does not appear on its own layer, it appears as pixels on the background layer and cannot be edited.

The Options bar with the Type tool selected

The Options bar in Text Editing mode

Creating Paragraph Type

When you work with Paragraph type, you define the width of the column of text. The text wraps to a new line when it reaches the edge of the type bounding box.

If you enter more type than can fit in the type bounding box, an overflow symbol appears in the bottom right corner of the bounding box. Make the type smaller, or the box bigger to see all the type.

To resize the type bounding box, select the Type tool, click on the type layer in the Layers palette, then click in the text itself. Drag a resize handle to change the size of the text area.

1 To create Paragraph type, select the Type tool. You can create settings for the type using options in the Options bar, or the Character and Paragraph palettes before you enter the type, or you can format the type after you enter it.

2 Position your cursor at one corner of the type area you want to create. Drag diagonally to define the size of the type's bounding box.

3 With the Type tool selected, you can hold down Alt, then click in the image to access the Paragraph Text Size dialogue box. Enter values for Width and Height, then click OK.

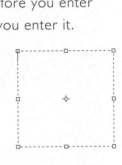

4 Enter text using the keyboard. Text wraps when it reaches the edge of the type bounding box. Press Enter (Win), Return (Mac) on the main keyboard only when you want to begin a new paragraph.

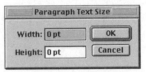

5 Click on the Commit/OK button in the Options bar to commit the type layer. This takes Photoshop out of Text Editing mode and you can now perform other tasks on the image. The type appears on its own layer.

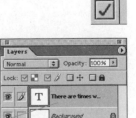

Editing and Selecting Type

To edit type you must go into Text Editing mode. To make changes to the formatting of text you must first be able to highlight or select the text on which you want to work. You can then make changes to the character/paragraph settings.

Editing Text

| To edit text select the Type tool. Click on the type layer in the Layers palette, then click in the type to place the text insertion point where you want to add or delete characters. Or, click directly into the text you want to change.

Editable Type layers are represented by the 'T' icon in the Layers palette. Double-click the 'T' icon to select all the text on a type layer.

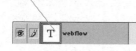

2 This takes Photoshop into Text Editing mode. Make changes using the keyboard as necessary.

3 Click the Commit button in the Options bar to accept the changes you make and to leave Text Editing mode. Click the Cancel button in the Options bar if you do not want to keep the changes.

Selecting Text

Before making changes to settings for existing text, you must first select the range of text you want to change. You can select all the text on a type layer, or specific ranges of text.

| To select a specific range of text, first select the Type tool. Click on the type layer in the layers palette, or click directly into the text.

2 Click and drag across the text to highlight a specific range of characters, from a single character, to a word, to all visible text.

There are times when one does not quite know what one is going to type, so you end up typing something like this.

To reposition type, select the Move tool, make sure the type layer is selected in the Layers palette, then drag the type layer as you would to reposition any other layer.

3 Click in the text to place the text insertion point. This defines the start of the text you want to highlight. Move the cursor (do not press and drag), then hold down Shift and click to define the end of the range of text.

There are times when one does not quite know what one is going to type, so you end up typing something like this.

The next paragrph follows on

4 Double-click on a word to highlight one word. Triple-click to highlight a line of text. Click four times to select a paragraph.

Double-click the Type layer icon in the Layers palette to select all the text in the type layer.

5 In Text Editing mode, use Command/Ctrl+A to select all text on the layer, or choose Select > All.

There are times when *one does not quite know* what one is going to type, so you end up typing something like this.

The next paragrph

6 With the appropriate range of text highlighted you can then make changes to the settings. The changes you make apply to the highlighted text only.

Character Settings

You can choose Window > Show Character to show the Character/Paragraph palette, or you can click the Palettes button in the Options bar if you have the Type tool selected.

You can use options in the Options bar when the Type tool is selected, or in the Character palette to change the settings for selected text.

Font

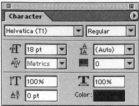

Use the Font pop-up to choose from the list of fonts available on your system. Choose a style such as Bold, Italic, from the Font Style pop-up.

Make sure you have selected a range of text before you make changes to Character settings.

Size

Enter a value in the Size box to change the size of your type. Points are the default unit of measurement for type in Photoshop.

Leading

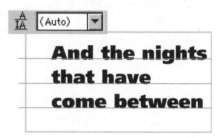

Leading controls the distance from one baseline of type to the next. Enter a leading value in points in the leading entry box. Photoshop applies a default leading value of 125% of the type size you have selected if you leave the leading set to (Auto).

If you are uncertain about which control is which in the Character palette, rest your cursor on the icon to the left of the entry box until the tool tip label appears.

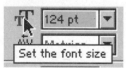

Kerning and Tracking

In the Character you can create settings for Kerning and Tracking. Metrics, the default, uses the built-in pair kerning table for the font.

To kern character pairs, click between the characters in the text entry window to place the text insertion bar. You can enter a value in the  Kerning entry box or use the pop-up to choose a preset value. Negative values move characters closer together. Positive values move characters apart. Press Enter/Return to accept the changes made in the dialogue.

A Faux style allows you to simulate a font style which doesn't exist on your system. You cannot apply Faux Bold to warped type.

To change the colour of selected text, click the colour box in the Options bar or in the Character palette. (See page 64 for further information on using the Colour Picker palette.)

2 For Tracking, highlight a range of text you want to track. Enter a value in the Tracking entry box, or use the pop-up.

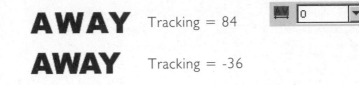

AWAY Tracking = 84

AWAY Tracking = -36

Baseline Shift

The Baseline Shift control allows you to move highlighted characters above or below their original baseline to create a variety of effects.

You must commit changes to type before you can make other changes to the image.

1 To baseline shift characters, in Text Editing mode make sure you highlight the characters you want to shift.

2 Enter a positive value to baseline shift upwards, enter a negative value to baseline shift downward.

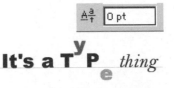

Anti-Aliasing

In most instances, fractional character widths provide the best spacing for type. Switch off the Fractional Widths option when working with type below 20 points that is to be viewed on screen. If you leave the option selected, type characters may run together when displayed on a monitor screen.

Access the Fractional Widths option from the pop-up menu in the Character palette.

The anti-aliased setting in the Options bar creates type with a slightly soft edge. It does this by blurring the pixels that form the edge of the type. Use this option to avoid unnecessary jagged edges, unless you are working with very small type. Anti-aliasing text can help the type to blend into its background. Text that is not anti-aliased can look jagged. Choose an amount of anti-aliasing from the Anti-Alias pop-up in the Options bar.

Type at very small sizes can appear blurred if anti-aliasing is applied.

Paragraph Settings

The controls in the Paragraph palette are most useful when you are working with Paragraph type consisting of one or more paragraphs. Choose Window > Show Paragraph if the palette is not already showing.

With the Type tool selected, you can click the Palettes button in the Options bar to show the Paragraph palette.

| Before you can apply Paragraph settings you must highlight the range of text on which you want to work. (See pages 138–139)

Alignment

Select the type layer in the Layers palette to apply settings to all paragraphs on that layer.

| To change the alignment for selected paragraphs, or a complete layer, click on one of the alignment buttons: Left, Right, Centre, in the Paragraph palette or Options bar.

To set an indent in millimetres, enter a number, followed by mm.

2 Choose one of the Justify alignment options to justify type so that both edges of the column are straight. You cannot justify Point type. The variations for justified type affect how the last line of a paragraph is treated. Rest the cursor on the icon for a tool tip label.

Indents

Use the Hyphenate option to allow or disallow hyphenation in selected text.

☑ Hyphenate

| To set a Left, Right or First line indent for selected paragraphs, enter a value in the appropriate entry box.

Space Before, Space After

| To create additional space above and/or below a paragraph or range of selected paragraphs, enter a value in the Space Before, Space After entry boxes.

Masked Type

In essence, the Masked Type option creates a complex selection – a selection in the shape of type. This can be powerful and flexible when you want to show images through the shape of letterforms.

Because you do not get a preview of type settings in the image window when you use the Type Mask tool, create a standard type layer with the type settings you want before you use the Type Mask tool. Settings you create for the standard layer in the Type Tool dialogue box are remembered. Delete the standard type layer afterwards.

With the Type Mask tool still selected, position your cursor inside the selection border, then click and drag to reposition the selection area if necessary.

The Masked Type option creates a selection. You can move, copy, fill or stroke the masked type selection as you can for any other selection.

1 Select the Type tool. Click the Masked Type button in the Options bar. Position your cursor on the image where you want the type to start. Click. This sets the text insertion point. A translucent colour mask appears across the image.

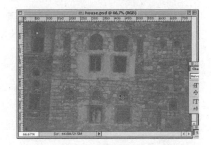

2 Enter text on the keyboard. As you type the coloured mask becomes transparent in the letterforms to indicate the type mask selection. Click the Commit button in the Options bar to create the selection.

3 A type selection appears in the image window. Notice that the Type Mask tool does not create a new layer.

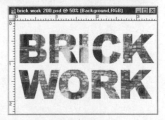

4 You can now drag the selection to a new image window, create a new layer from the selection or use any commands that you would typically use on a selection.

Type and Layer Styles

Layer Styles can be applied to type layers whilst the type layer remains an editable-type layer.

1. To apply a Layer Style to a type layer, first click on the type layer to make it active.

2. Choose Layer > Layer Styles. Select a style from the style sub-menu. Create settings in the Layer Style dialogue box. When you OK the dialogue box, the layer in the layers palette now has a [T] and an [f] icon indicating that it is an editable-type layer with a layer effect applied. (See page 125 for information on working with layer styles. See page 138 for information on working with editable-type layers.)

Yemen

The editable type layer with its layer style separated from the Background layer.

Paths

An understanding of paths in Photoshop is essential for creating cutouts for use in page layout applications such as QuarkXPress and Adobe PageMaker. Paths can also be used to create accurate selections.

You can save paths with the image file in Photoshop format, convert paths into selections, or convert selections into paths. You can also export paths to Adobe Illustrator.

Covers

Chapter Eleven

Converting Selections to Paths

A quick and convenient technique for creating a path is to make a selection, convert the selection into a work path, and then into a path.

Use Window > Show Paths to show the Paths palette.

1 First make a selection using any of the selection tools. Then, use the Paths palette pop-up menu and choose Make Work Path, or click the Make Work Path icon.

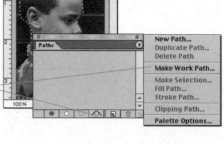

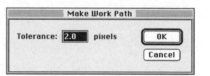

You can only have one work path in the Paths palette at any one time. A work path is a temporary path only. For a path to be saved when you save your file, you must first save the path (see step 4, on the next page).

2 The Make Work Path dialogue box appears if you use the Make Work Path command. Specify a tolerance value (from 0.5– 10). (If you click the Make Work Path icon, the last-used settings from the dialogue box are applied automatically.) The tolerance value controls how closely the path conforms to the selection. A low tolerance value creates a path that follows the selection tightly, but creates a greater number of points. A high tolerance value produces a path that follows the selection more loosely, but with fewer points.

3 OK the dialogue box. A work path appears in the Paths palette, along with a thumbnail of the path. The selection disappears.

4 Choose Save Path from the
pop-up menu if you want
to save this path before
making any adjustments to it. Enter a name. OK the dialogue
box. The new path appears in the palette, replacing the
work path.

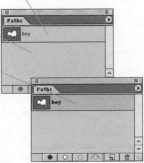

5 To hide the path, click in empty
space in the Paths palette. To show
the path, click on the path name to
select it. The path highlights.

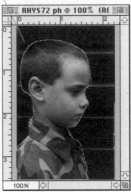

Converting Paths to Selections
You can also convert a path into a selection. This is useful
when you want a very accurate selection.

To convert a path into a selection, click on the path in the
Paths palette to highlight it. Then choose Make Selection
from the pop-up
menu, or click the
Make Selection icon.

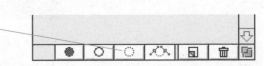

Creating Paths Using the Pen Tool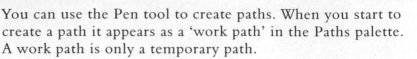

You can use the Pen tool to create paths. When you start to create a path it appears as a 'work path' in the Paths palette. A work path is only a temporary path.

The Pen tool creates anchor points which are connected by straight lines or curved segments. You can use the other tools in the Paths tool group to modify a path by adding, deleting or moving anchor points, and by changing the nature of the point, from smooth to corner and vice versa. You can also edit curved segments by dragging the Bezier direction points.

Use the Paths pop-up menu to create a new path before you use the Pen tool to automatically save the path without going through the intermediary stage of a work path.

1 To create a path, select the Pen tool

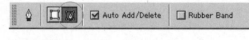

in the Toolbox. Make sure the Create Work Path icon is selected. You can select the Rubber band option in the Options bar if you want to see a preview of the line segments as you draw.

2 Position your cursor where you want to start drawing the path, then click, release the button, move the mouse and click again to create a straight line segment. Continue moving your cursor and clicking to create further straight line segments.

You can press the Delete key to delete the last anchor point. If you press Delete twice, you will delete the entire path.

Use the Freeform Pen tool to create a path by clicking and dragging the mouse. This is similar to drawing with a pencil. You have no control over where Photoshop places anchor points, but you can easily edit the path after it is drawn.

3 Alternatively, you can click and drag to set an anchor point and create direction lines for a curve segment.

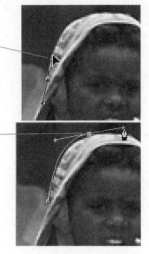

4 Then, release the button and move the cursor, and again click and drag to create the next anchor point with direction lines.

5 Continue in this way to create the path you want.

You can only have one work path in a file. It is a good idea to save the path and give it a name, so you do not delete it accidentally by creating another work path. See page 147 for details on saving your work path.

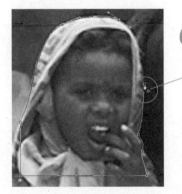

6 Position the Pen tool cursor at the start point. Notice the cursor now has a small circle attached to it. Click to create a closed path. The path will appear in the Paths palette with the default title of Work Path.

Provided that Auto Add/ Delete is selected in the Options bar, you can use the Pen tool to add and delete anchor points. The tool cursor changes intelligently, depending on whether you position the cursor on an anchor point or a line segment.

7 To create an open path, follow the techniques outlined above, but instead of clicking back at the start point, click on the Pen tool in the Toolbox to finish the path. This is now an open path to which you could, for example, apply a stroke.

Showing and Selecting Paths and Points

Use the following techniques for selecting, deselecting and deleting paths.

1 To select a path, first you have to show it. To do this, click the path name in the Paths palette. The path now shows in the image window.

2 To select the path, select the Direct Selection tool (the hollow arrow). Click on the path to make it active. You now see the curve and line segments together with the anchor points that form the path.

A selected anchor point is a solid square; a non-selected point is a hollow square.

3 Click on the anchor point of a curve segment to select the point and display the direction points.

4 To select and move an entire path, show the path, then hold down Alt and click on the path. Using the Direct Selection tool, position your cursor on an anchor point or curve segment, then click and drag to reposition the path. To deselect a path, click away from the path using the Direct Selection tool. The path still shows, but is not selected.

To improve the clarity of these screen shots, the path has been moved 1 pixel away from the edge of the image.

5 To delete a path, with a point or line segment of the path selected press Delete twice. Alternatively, with the entire path selected, press Delete once. You can also drag the path name onto the Wastebasket icon in the Paths palette.

Add, Delete and Convert Points

To achieve a precise path, you often need to add points and delete points on a path.

For a smooth point, when you drag one of the direction points, the other point balances it to maintain a smooth curve at the anchor point.

1 To add a point, make sure the path is selected, select the Add Point tool from the Pen Tool group, position your cursor on the path and then click. If you click on a curve segment you automatically get an anchor point with direction points. If you click on a straight line segment, you get just an anchor point.

2 To delete a point, make sure the path is selected, select the Delete Point tool, position your cursor on an existing anchor point, then click. The path redraws without the point.

A corner point is one which allows a sharp change of direction at the anchor point. Notice that for a corner point, when you drag one of the direction points, the other point is not affected. You have complete, independent control over each direction point.

3 To convert a smooth point into a corner point, select an anchor point with the Direct Selection tool. Select the Convert Anchor Point tool, position your cursor on a direction point, then click and drag. Use the Direct Selection tool to make any further changes to the direction points.

The Add Anchor Point tool cursor appears as a hollow arrow until you position it on a path. It then becomes the Pen cursor with an additional plus (+) symbol. Similarly, the Delete Anchor point tool cursor only appears when you position the cursor on an existing anchor point.

4 To convert anchor points on straight line segments into smooth points, select the Convert Anchor Point tool, position your cursor on the anchor point, then click and drag. Direction lines appear around the point. Use the Direct Selection tool to make any further changes to the points.

5 To convert a smooth point into a corner point without direction lines, select the Convert Anchor Point tool, then click on an anchor point.

Creating Corner Points

As you use the Pen tool to create paths, you can draw corner points as you go, in combination with straight line segments and smooth points. In many instances, a smooth point cannot create the shape of the path you want.

A corner point allows a sharp change of direction at the anchor point. In a corner point, the direction points can be manipulated independently. This is what makes them essential to create paths that require sharp changes of direction.

The paths in these screen shots have been moved one pixel away from the edge of the leaf so that they display more clearly. When you create a clipping path, it is best to position the path a pixel or so inside the shape you want to cut out, to avoid unwanted edge pixels being included. Unwanted edge pixels are sometimes referred to as 'edge tear'.

1 To draw a corner point, click and drag as you would to set a smooth point. Concentrate on getting the shape of the path coming into the point correct. Release the mouse button.

2 Position your cursor on the anchor point, hold down Alt, then click and drag off the point. This converts the point to a corner point. You are now controlling the direction of the outgoing curve segment. As you drag the second direction point, notice that it no longer has any effect on the incoming direction point.

3 Move your cursor to a new position, then continue drawing either smooth or corner points.

Editing Points

Paths invariably need to be modified and fine-tuned to produce the result you require.

1   To edit a smooth point, make sure the path is selected, then click on the anchor point to select it. Direction points appear either side of the anchor point. Direction points control the shape and length of a curve segment.

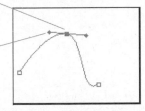

2   When you drag a direction point of a smooth anchor point, as you change the angle of one side, the other direction point moves to balance the point you are moving. This ensures the curve is always smooth through the anchor point.

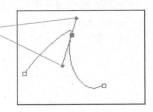

3   The further away from the anchor point you drag a direction point, the longer the associated curve segment becomes. As the curve segment is anchored at the anchor points at either end, this causes the curve segment to bow out more. Bring the direction point closer to the anchor point and the curve segment becomes shorter.

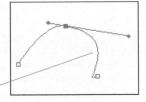

4   When you drag direction points on a corner anchor point, each moves totally independently of the other, allowing a sharp change of direction at the point.

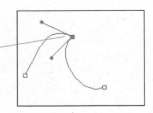

Exporting Clipping Paths

Create a clipping path when you want to create transparent areas in an image you intend to use in an application such as Adobe Illustrator, QuarkXPress or Adobe InDesign.

A clipping path makes areas of the image outside the path transparent, allowing you to see past the outline of the image to the background on which the image is placed.

Flatness allows a PostScript printer to create less memory-intensive paths at output. If you use too high a flatness value, you get an approximate path that does not accurately conform to the path you created.

For high-resolution printing (1200–2400 dpi) a flatness value of 8 to 10 should be acceptable. Use a value of 1 to 3 for low resolution printing (300–600 dpi). Leave the field blank to use the printer's default setting. This usually produces good results with most images.

1 Create a saved path (see page 147). If you have more than one path in the Paths palette, make sure you select the appropriate path. Use the pop-up palette menu to select Clipping Path.

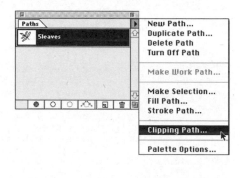

2 Use the Path pop-up to specify a different path to make into a clipping path if necessary. Enter a flatness value.

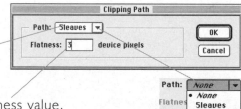

3 When you have saved a clipping path, you need to save the file in EPS or TIFF file format for output. Choose File > Save As. In the Save As dialogue box, give the file a name and specify where you want to save it.

4 Choose Photoshop EPS or TIFF from the Format pop-up. Click Save. Clipping

Paths saved with the image are automatically exported with the file when you save in Photoshop EPS or TIFF file format.

Remember to convert the file to an appropriate mode – e.g. CMYK – before you save the file in EPS format.

5 See the section on saving in Photoshop EPS format (page 46) for information on Preview and encoding options.

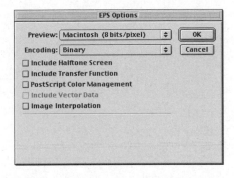

Select a TIFF preview option if you intend to use the image on the Windows platform.

6 When you import the file into a QuarkXPress page, the clipping path hides areas of the image outside the clipping path. The second version of the same image on this Quark page has a white background and does not have a clipping path.

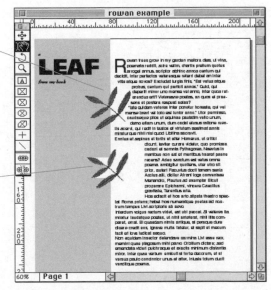

Save a file with a clipping path in Photoshop EPS format if you are printing the file to a PostScript output device.

Exporting Paths to Adobe Illustrator

Exporting a path to Illustrator is useful when you want to place type along a path originated in Photoshop. The type can then be saved as an EPS file in Illustrator and placed back into Photoshop. This is useful because Photoshop does not have as much flexibility for creating type effects as Illustrator.

1 To export a path to Adobe Illustrator, choose File > Export > Paths to Illustrator. In the Export Paths dialogue box, change the name if necessary but leave the automatically generated .ai extension to distinguish the file. If your Photoshop document has more than one saved path, use the Write pop-up to choose the path you want to export. Click Save.

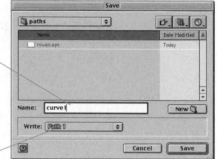

You can use the Export Paths to Illustrator command and then open the file in Macromedia FreeHand if you do not have Adobe Illustrator.

2 Use File > Open in Adobe Illustrator to import the path and place type along it. Save the Illustrator file in EPS format.

When you open exported paths in Adobe Illustrator, the crop marks indicate the dimensions of the original Photoshop image.

3 Place the Illustrator EPS into the Photoshop document that you originally exported the path from. (See page 43, Chapter Three.)

4 Position the EPS bounding box, resize the EPS if necessary, then press Return/Enter to place the text from Illustrator onto a new layer.

Channels and Masks

The Channels palette stores colour information about an image and can also be used to store selections on a permanent basis.

Masks are created and used in a variety of ways in Photoshop. The basic principle of masks is that you use them to protect areas of an image from editing that you carry out on the unmasked areas of the image.

Use Quick Mask mode when you don't want to save the mask for future use. Layer masks control how different areas of pixels on a layer are hidden or revealed.

Covers

Chapter Twelve

Quick Mask Mode

In Quick Mask mode you create a 50% red, semi-transparent overlay. This overlay represents the protected area of the image. The overlay is similar in concept to a traditional rubylith mask. Quick Mask mode is particularly useful because you can see both the image and the mask as you create and fine-tune the mask.

You can make a rough selection first, then go into Quick Mask mode and edit the mask further if necessary.

1 To create a quick mask, click the Quick Mask Mode icon. Make sure that the default foreground and background colours are black and white respectively.

2 Show the Brushes palette and choose a brush size. Use a hard-edged brush for most control. Select a painting tool and drag across your image to 'paint' in the mask. Painting with black adds to the mask. Although you see through the 50% red mask, the pixels covered by the mask are completely protected.

Painting with grey or any other colour creates a semi-transparent or partial mask.

3 To remove areas from the mask you can use the Eraser tool, or paint with white.

4 When you are satisfied with your mask, click the Standard Mode button. This turns the areas of the image that were not part of your quick mask into a selection. You can now make changes to the selected areas (in this example the Blur filter has been applied), leaving the areas that were the quick mask unchanged.

The Channels Palette

The Channels palette (Window > Show Channels) shows a breakdown of the colour components that combine to make up the composite colour image that you work with most of the time on-screen.

You can change the display of channels from greyscale to the colour they represent by choosing Edit > Preferences > Display and Cursor. Select Colour Channels in Colour.

For example, in RGB mode, there are four channels – the composite image (all the other channels combined), and then a channel each for the red, green and blue colour components of the image. In CMYK mode, there are five channels.

Using the Channels palette you can be selective about which of the colour components in your image you change.

To switch to a specific channel, click the channel name in the Channels palette. The channel highlights to indicate that it is selected. The image window changes according to the channel you chose.

Indexed Colour mode, Greyscale mode and Bitmap mode all have only one channel.

2 You can view additional channels by clicking the eye icon for a channel. The image window changes, but your editing remains limited to the selected channel.

3 Click on the composite channel to return to normal image-editing view.

Saving and Loading Selections

Because you can only have one 'active' selection in an image at any one time, the facility to store a selection which can be reloaded later is vital, especially if the selection is complex and took some time to create. You save selections as an extra channel in the Channels palette. These extra channels are referred to as 'alpha channels'.

An alpha channel is an 8-bit greyscale channel, which means that every time you save a selection as a channel, you are adding to the file size of your image.

Saving Selections

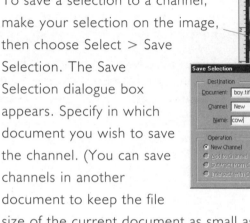

1   To save a selection to a channel, make your selection on the image, then choose Select > Save Selection. The Save Selection dialogue box appears. Specify in which document you wish to save the channel. (You can save channels in another document to keep the file size of the current document as small as possible.) Leave the Channel pop-up on New. Enter a name for the channel. Click OK. Alternatively, make your selection and then click the Save Selection icon in the Channels palette.

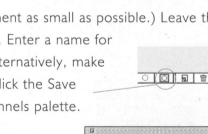

You can only save an alpha channel with a picture in Photoshop, TIFF or PICT (RGB) file formats.

2   In the Channels palette, you will see an extra channel. This is the new 'alpha channel'. An alpha channel is a greyscale channel.

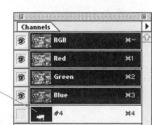

3   When you have saved a selection to an alpha channel you can freely deselect the selection in your image, as you can now reselect exactly the same area at any time using the alpha channel.

File formats that can retain alpha channel information when you save include: Photoshop, PDF, PICT and TIFF.

Loading Selections

Use the following process to reselect an area using the alpha channel:

1 To load a channel selection as a selection on the image, make sure the composite image is displayed. You can do this by clicking on the topmost channel name in the Channels palette. Then choose Select > Load Selection. The Load Selection dialogue box appears.

2 Use the Channel pop-up menu to specify which channel you want to load. Select an operation as appropriate. The operations allow you to control how the selection you are about to

load interacts with any existing selection in the image – adding to it, subtracting from it or intersecting with it. Click OK.

When you are working in Quick Mask mode, you can turn the quick mask into an alpha channel by dragging the quick mask entry that appears in the Channels palette onto the New Channel icon.

3 Alternatively, using the Channels palette, drag the channel you want to load onto the Load Selection icon.

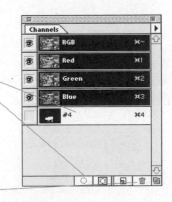

4 To delete a channel, drag the channel name onto the Wastebasket icon at the bottom of the palette.

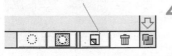

Editing Alpha Channel Masks

You can display an alpha channel without loading it onto the image as a selection. You can then edit the mask by painting with black, white or grey.

1 To display an alpha channel, choose Windows > Show Channels to display the Channels palette. Click on the alpha channel you want to display. The channel name , and an eye icon in the left column of the palette indicates that this is the visible channel.

2 The image window changes from the composite view to a greyscale representation of the mask. The white area represents the selection and the black portions represent the protected areas.

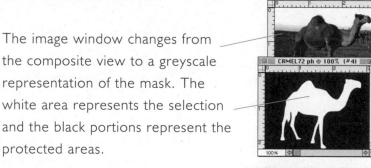

If you paint with grey you can create a semi-transparent mask.

3 To edit a selection channel, select a painting tool and brush size. Click the Default Colours icon if necessary, to change the foreground colour to black. Paint with black to remove areas from the selection. Paint with white on any black portion of the mask to add it to the selection.

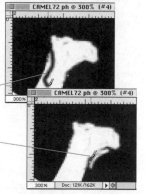

Make sure you do not have a selection showing (marching ants) before you attempt to modify or edit the selection mask channel.

Another useful technique for editing a selection mask is to view a mask and image simultaneously by turning the alpha channel selection into a coloured mask (very much like using Quick Mask mode) and then reshaping the mask by painting with black, white or shades of grey.

Reshaping Masks

1 To reshape a mask, ensure you don't have an active selection on your image. Click on the alpha channel in the Channels palette to select it. It highlights and the eye icon shows on the left. The image window now displays the greyscale selection channel mask. Notice that the eye icon disappears from the Composite RGB channel and from the individual Red, Green and Blue channels.

 Typically, when you edit masks, you will paint with black or white, with the mode set to Normal and an opacity of 100%. However, you can reduce the opacity or pressure setting in order to create a partial mask.

2 Click in the currently empty eye icon position for the Composite channel. The eye appears for the Composite channel and in the individual Red, Green and Blue ones. The Composite channel now also shows in the image window but only the alpha channel is selected – indicated by the highlight.

 Make sure that the eye icon for an alpha channel mask is not selected, then click the Composite channel when you want to return to the standard editing view.

3 The image window now changes in appearance. The selection area appears as normal, whilst the protected or masked portions of the image have a quick mask-type transparent film applied.

4 Select the Paintbrush or Pencil tool. Paint with white to remove areas of the image from the mask (to enlarge the unmasked area). Paint with black to add portions of the image to the mask.

Layer Masks

Use layer masks to hide or reveal areas of a layer. A layer mask is extremely useful because you can use it to try out effects without actually changing the pixels on the layer. When you have achieved the result you want, you can apply the mask as a permanent change. If you are not satisfied, you can discard the mask without having permanently affected the pixels on the layer.

For information on creating layers, see Chapter Nine. For information on using filters, see Chapter Fourteen.

This example begins with an image with two layers. The background layer is the original scan; the other layer was   using the Render > Clouds filter.

1 To create a layer mask for the clouds layer, first click on the layer to make it active.

Choose Layer > Add Layer Mask > Reveal All. Reveal All means that all the pixels in the layer are visible. The Clouds layer now completely obscures the background layer.

You can only have one layer mask per layer.

2 In the Layers palette, the layer mask is active, indicated by the mask icon next to the eye icon. Click on the layer thumbnail to make the layer active (the paintbrush

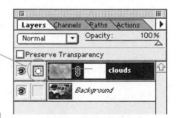

icon indicates that you can now work directly on the layer). Click on the layer mask icon to continue editing the mask.

3 With the layer mask selected, make sure that the foreground colour is set to black. Choose a painting tool and start painting. Painting with black hides pixels on the clouds layer, revealing pixels on the Background layer.

You can paint with shades of grey to partially hide pixels on the clouds layer.

4 Pixels on the clouds layer are not permanently erased when you paint with black. Paint with white to show pixels on the clouds layer – in effect hiding pixels on the background layer. (If you choose Layer > Add Layer Mask > Hide All, you start with the opposite scenario to the above. Now all the pixels on the clouds layer are hidden. Paint with white to reveal pixels on the clouds layer, paint with black to hide them.)

5 To temporarily switch off the Layer mask, choose Layer > Disable Mask, or hold down Shift, then click on the Layer Mask icon. To reactivate the mask, choose Layer > Enable Layer Mask, or hold down Shift, then click again on the Layer Mask icon.

6 To apply the layer mask as a permanent change, choose Layer > Remove Layer Mask > Apply. To discard the layer mask, without affecting pixels on the layer, choose Layer > Remove Layer Mask > Discard.

7 Or, drag the Layer Mask icon (not the layer icon) onto the Wastebasket icon in the bottom of the palette. Click Apply or Discard. Once you apply a layer mask you lose the flexibility of making further changes – the effect is fixed. Click Discard only if you want to delete the mask.

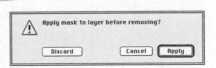

Channel and Quick Mask Options

The Channel Options dialogue box and the Quick Mask Options dialogue box allow you to control the colour of a mask and whether the protected or unprotected area of the image is coloured with the overlay.

1 To change channel options, double-click the alpha channel name. Alternatively, with the alpha channel selected, use the Channels pop-up menu to choose Channel Options.

2 In the Channel Options dialogue box you can enter a new name for the channel. You can also choose Selected Areas to reverse the way in which the colour will apply. In other words, masked (protected) areas will appear white, while the selection area (unprotected) will appear black.

3 To change the colour used to represent the masked (protected) area and its opacity, click the Colour box and choose a new colour from the colour picker.

4 To change the settings for a quick mask, double-click either the Quick Mask Mode icon or the Standard Mode icon, then make the appropriate changes in the dialogue box that appears.

Colour Correction Techniques

Colour correction involves making changes to the overall brightness and contrast in an image and also the colour balance to compensate for any tonal deficiencies and colour casts in the original scan.

You should bear in mind that although colour corrections can improve the overall appearance of an image, inevitably some colour values will be lost – certain pixels in the original scan that were different colours will end up remapped to the same colour.

Covers

Chapter Thirteen

The Brightness/Contrast Command

The Brightness/Contrast command provides the least complicated controls for changing overall brightness and contrast levels in an image. It does not allow you to make changes to individual colour channels; it makes the same adjustment to every pixel across the entire tonal range of the image.

1   To change brightness and contrast, for an entire image, or for a selection, choose Image > Adjust > Brightness/Contrast.

Choose Image > Adjust > Auto Contrast (Ctrl/Command +Alt+Shift+L) to automatically adjust the contrast in the image. Highlights should appear lighter and shadows darker resulting in an overall improvement in the image.

Auto Contrast does not adjust individual channels in an image. It makes highlights appear lighter and shadows darker, by mapping the lightest and darkest pixels in the image to white and black respectively.

2   Drag the Brightness and Contrast sliders to the right or left, or enter a value in the entry boxes (-100 to +100). OK the dialogue box.

3   If you are making adjustments to a selection, click the Preview button to see, on-screen, the result of the settings you choose.

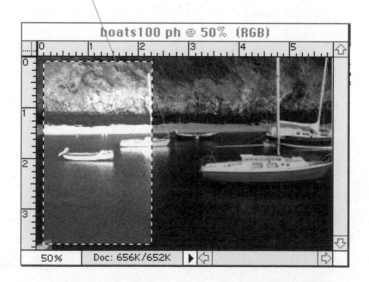

The Auto Levels Command

Auto Levels allows you to adjust brightness and contrast automatically. Auto Levels examines each colour channel independently and changes the darkest pixels to black and the lightest pixels to white, then redistributes the remaining shades of grey between these two points.

Auto Levels works best on images that have a reasonably even distribution of tonal values throughout the image, as it redistributes pixels based on white and black points, with a tendency to increase contrast. This generally produces good results, but Auto Levels does not allow the precision of manual adjustments that you can make using the Levels and Curves dialogue boxes.

Auto Levels adjusts each colour channel in the image individually. As a result, it may remove or introduce colour casts.

1 To apply Auto Levels to an image, choose Image > Adjust > Auto Levels. (Use Edit > Undo if you do not like the result.)

2 You can also use the Auto Levels command from within the Levels and Curves dialogue boxes. Click the Auto button.

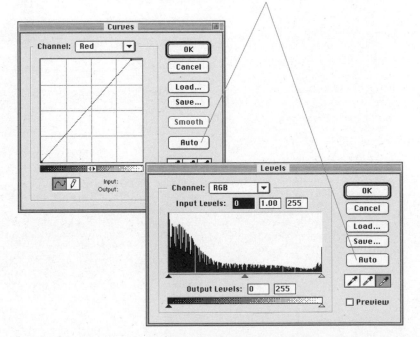

The Levels Dialogue Box

Use the Levels dialogue box (Image > Adjust > Levels) to adjust the tonal balance for colour and greyscale images. You can adjust highlight, shadow and midtone ranges for a selection or an entire image, or you can make changes to individual channels only.

Input Levels

The Input Levels sliders and entry boxes allow you to improve the contrast in a 'flat' image.

The most flexible way of working with Levels, Curves and Colour Balance is to set up Adjustment layers. Adjustment layers allow you to readjust settings in the respective dialogue boxes until you are satisfied with the result.

1 Use the Channel pop-up menu to select a channel. If you do not select an individual channel, you can work on the composite image and affect all channels.

2 To darken an image, drag the solid black slider to the right. Alternatively, enter an appropriate value in the leftmost Input Levels entry box. This maps or clips pixels to black. For example, if you drag the black slider to 15, all pixels with an original value between 0 and 15 become black. The result is a darker image.

Dragging either or both the black or white sliders inwards has the effect of increasing contrast in the image.

3 To lighten an image, drag the hollow, white Input Levels slider to the left. Alternatively, enter an appropriate value in the rightmost Input Levels entry box. The result is to map or clip pixels to white. For example, if you drag the white slider to 245, all pixels with an original value between 245 and 255 become white. The result is a lighter image.

Gamma

The grey triangle and the middle Input Levels entry box control the Gamma value in the image. The Gamma value is the brightness level of mid-grey pixels in the image.

When you OK the Levels dialogue box, you can use Edit > Undo/ Redo a number of times to evaluate the changes.

1 To lighten midtones, drag the grey slider to the left, or increase the Gamma value in the Input Levels entry box above the default setting of 1.00.

2 To darken midtones, drag the grey slider to the right, or decrease the Gamma value in the Input Levels entry box.

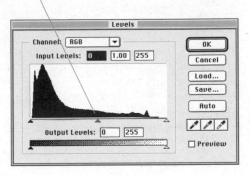

Output Levels

You can use the Output Levels entry boxes or sliders to decrease the amount of contrast in an image.

1 Drag the black Output Levels slider to the right to lighten the image and reduce the contrast.

See page 169 for an explanation of Auto Levels and the Auto button.

2 Drag the white Output Levels slider to the left to darken the image and reduce the contrast.

The Curves Dialogue Box

The Curves dialogue box (Image > Adjust > Curves) offers the most versatile set of controls for making tonal adjustments in an image. The central brightness graph in the dialogue box displays the original and adjusted brightness values for pixels in the image. The graph is a straight line from 0 (black) to 255 (white), before any adjustments are made – input and output values for pixels are the same.

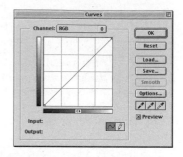

You should be careful not to click on the brightness bar at the bottom of the Curves dialogue box accidentally.

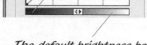

The default brightness bar starts black and graduates to white. In this state, the brightness curve indicates the brightness values of colours in the image; the brightness curve starts at 0, for black, and moves to 255, for white.

The horizontal axis of the graph represents the original or input values, the vertical axis represents the output or adjusted values. By adjusting the brightness curve, you are remapping the brightness values of pixels in the image.

1   To add a point to the curve, select the Point tool. (This is the default selection.) Click on the curve. (You can add up to fifteen points.) Drag the point(s) around to edit the curve. Alternatively, click at a point in the graph and the curve will change according to where you clicked.

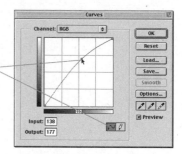

2   To delete a point, click on a point to select it, then press the Delete/Backspace key. You can also drag it outside the Brightness graph.

3   To lighten an image, select the Point tool, position your cursor near the midpoint of the graph, then click to place a new point. Click and drag this point upwards.

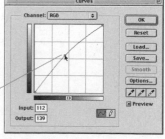

Hold down Alt, then click on the Reset button (previously Cancel) to restore the original settings in the dialogue box.

4 To darken an image, select the Point tool, position your cursor near the midpoint of the graph, then click to place a point. Drag the point downwards.

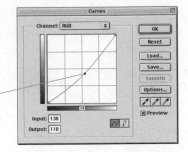

5 To increase the contrast in an image, place a point at roughly the ¼ tone part of the graph and drag this upwards to lighten the highlights. Next, place a point at roughly the ¾ tone part of the graph. Drag this downward to darken the shadow areas. The result is to increase the contrast in the image by lightening the highlights and darkening the shadows, whilst leaving the midtones more or less untouched.

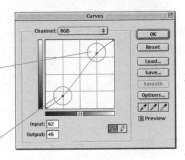

6 Reverse the setting in step 5 to decrease the contrast in an image.

7 To limit changes to the midtones and highlights, click on the graph to place a point at the ¾ tones. Place a point at the ¼ tones and drag this upwards. Reverse this procedure to change midtones and shadows without affecting highlights.

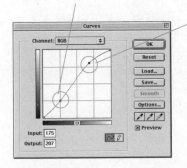

The Colour Balance Dialogue Box

Like the Brightness/Contrast command, the Colour Balance dialogue box provides general controls for correcting an overall colour cast in an image. As such, it provides the least complex method of colour correction.

The Colour Balance dialogue box works on the principle of complementary colours. If there is too much cyan in an image, you drag the Cyan–Red slider towards red to remove the cyan colour cast. If there is too much magenta, drag the Magenta–Green slider towards green.

Work on the composite view of an image when using the Colour Balance dialogue box.

You should use the Colour Balance dialogue box with caution, and only if your monitor is calibrated accurately, as you need to be certain that the colour adjustments you see on screen accurately represent colours at final output.

I   To adjust the colour balance of an image, choose Image > Adjust > Colour Balance. Click the Shadow, Midtone or Highlights radio button to specify the tonal range to which you want to make changes.

2   Drag the colour sliders to reduce/increase the amount of a colour in the image.

Preserve Luminosity

Select this option to prevent brightness values from changing as you change colour levels. This helps maintain the overall colour balance in the image.

Filters

Photoshop ships with more than 95 filters as standard. Filters add enormous creative flexibility and potential to image-manipulation, and they are well worth experimenting with.

You can use filters across an entire image, or you can apply them to selections to limit the results to specific areas. Filters cannot be applied to images in Bitmap or Indexed Colour mode.

Covers

Chapter Fourteen

Filter Controls

Many of the filters have standard controls, which are explained below.

2 Click and drag on the image in the Preview window to scroll around to preview different parts of the image. Alternatively, with the filter dialogue box active, position your cursor in the main image window – the cursor becomes a hollow box – then click to set the view in the Preview window.

1 Click the Preview check box to see the effect of your settings previewed in the main image window, as well as in the Preview window inside the filter dialogue box.

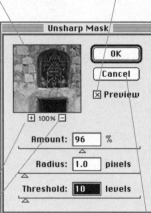

If you have the Preview box checked, click and hold on the Preview window inside the filter dialogue box to see the image without the filter settings applied.

3 Click the '+' or '–' buttons to zoom in or out on areas of the image. You can also use the Command + Spacebar (Mac) or Ctrl + Spacebar (Windows) keyboard shortcuts within the Preview window or the image window.

4 Hold down Alt and click the Reset button (previously Cancel) to revert to the original settings in the dialogue box.

5 After you OK a filter dialogue box, use Command + F (Mac) or Ctrl + F (Windows) to reapply the last-used filter and its settings.

A line flashing under the Preview check box means that Photoshop is still rendering the new settings.

Unsharp Mask and Sharpen Filters

These filters allow you to enhance the detail of your images.

Unsharp Mask

This is a powerful function which can help you to sharpen blurry images in specific areas. For example, if you rotate an image, or change the dimensions or resolution of the image, it may blur due to any interpolation that Photoshop applies. This can also happen when you convert from RGB to CMYK. Where the Unsharp Mask filter finds edges (areas where there is a high degree of contrast), it increases the contrast between adjacent pixels. The result is to create an apparent improvement in the focus of the image.

1 To use Unsharp Mask to sharpen an image, choose Filter > Sharpen > Unsharp mask. The Unsharp Mask dialogue box appears.

2 Adjust settings for Amount, Radius and Threshold. Click OK or press Return/Enter.

Amount – Use this to control the amount of sharpening applied to the edges (minimum = 1, maximum = 500). The picture will become pixelated if the amount is too high.

Values below 50% produce subtle effects; values between 50% and 250% produce moderate results, while values between 300% and 500% produce dramatic, exaggerated results.

The settings for Radius and Threshold need to be taken into account when setting the amount value (see the next page).

Radius – Radius controls the depth of pixels along the high-contrast edges that are changed.

A low radius value restricts the impact of the filter; higher values distribute the impact. Radius values of 2.0 or lower usually produce acceptable sharpening.

Threshold – Sets a level for the minimum amount of contrast between pixels an area must have before it will be modified. The Threshold value is the difference between two adjacent pixels – as measured in brightness levels – that must occur for Photoshop to recognise them as an edge.

On high-resolution images, use a Threshold value of 10 or higher to apply the sharpening effect to specific areas only.

High threshold values limit changes to areas where there is a high degree of colour difference. Use low values to apply the filter more generally throughout the image.

Sharpen and Sharpen More

Use the Sharpen and Sharpen More filters when an image becomes blurred after resampling. Both filters work by increasing contrast between adjacent pixels throughout the image or selection. Sharpen More has a more pronounced effect than Sharpen.

Sharpen Edges

This filter has a more specific effect, applying sharpening along high-contrast edges. In effect, it has a less global impact on a selection or image than Sharpen and Sharpen More.

Blur Filters

Blur More produces an effect roughly 3 times stronger than the Blur filter.

The Blur filters reduce the contrast between adjacent pixels along edges where considerable colour shifts occur, to create a softening, defocusing effect. Blurring produces the opposite effect to sharpening – which increases the contrast between adjacent pixels.

'Blur' and 'Blur More' blur a selection in preset amounts offering only a limited degree of control. For greater control when blurring you can use the Gaussian Blur option, which blurs according to a bell-shaped Gaussian distribution curve.

To Blur a Layer or Selection

I Create a selection if you want to limit the effect of the Blur filter to a specific area of your image. Choose Filter > Blur > Blur, or Filter > Blur > Blur More.

Angle = 0, Distance = 12

Angle = -45, Distance = 12

Angle = -53, Distance = 26

Motion Blur

You can use Motion Blur to create the effect of a moving subject or camera.

I To create a motion blur, make a selection, if required. Choose Filter > Blur > Motion Blur.

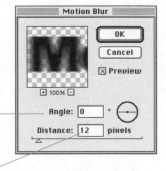

2 Enter a value in the Angle box, or drag the Angle indicator to specify the angle or direction of the blur. Enter a value in the Distance entry box to specify the distance in pixels for the blur effect. OK the dialogue box.

Radial Blur

Radial Blur creates the effect of zooming in as you take a picture.

| To create a radial blur, make a selection if required. Choose Filter > Blur > Radial Blur.

If you are working on a layer, make sure the Transparency lock is deselected if you want the blur to take effect along the edges of the layer's pixels. (See page 122)

2 Select a Blur Method and Quality, and specify an Amount (0–100). Click and drag in the Blur Centre window to specify the centre point for the zoom or spin effect. OK the dialogue box.

Amount – This value determines the distance pixels are moved to create the blur effect. Higher values produce more intense effects.

Zoom – Zoom creates a zoom-like blurring effect.

Spin – Spin rotates and blurs pixels around a central point.

Quality – Good and Best produce better, smoother results due to the interpolation methods used, but take longer.

Gaussian Blur

| Use Gaussian Blur to control the degree of blurring on the image. Gaussian Blur adds low frequency detail to the image or selection. Choose Filter > Blur > Gaussian. Use the Radius slider to adjust the amount of blurring.

Noise Filters

Add Noise

The Add Noise filter randomly distributes high-contrast pixels in an image, creating a grainy effect.

> To add noise, create a selection, or work on the entire image. Choose Filter > Noise > Add Noise. Specify Amount, Distribution and Monochromatic options.

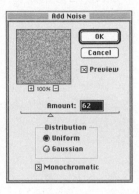

Amount – Determines the degree to which pixels are changed from their original colour. Enter a number from 1–999.

Uniform – Produces an even spread of pixels.

Gaussian – Produces a more dramatic result.

Monochromatic – Choose Monochromatic to distribute greyscale dots.

HOT TIP
You can use Add Noise to reduce banding in graduated fills.

HOT TIP
Add Noise is a good way to begin creating textured backgrounds.

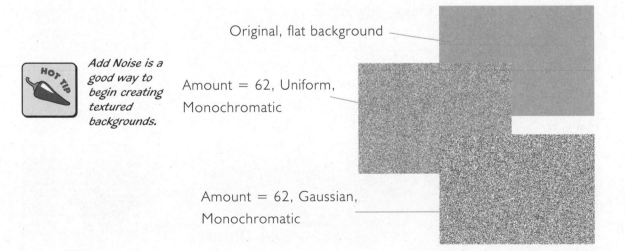

Original, flat background

Amount = 62, Uniform, Monochromatic

Amount = 62, Gaussian, Monochromatic

Dust & Scratches

Use the Dust & Scratches filter to remove small imperfections and blemishes in a scan caused by dust and scratches. The degree of success you have with this filter depends largely on the image or selection you apply it to.

Radius and Threshold settings are interdependent, and both are taken into account before changes are made.

| To remove dust and scratches, create a selection or work on the entire image. Choose Filters > Noise > Dust & Scratches. Specify Radius and Threshold settings. Click OK.

Radius – Determines how small a blemish must be for it to be worked upon by the filter. For example, at a radius of 3 pixels, the Dust & Scratches filter will not attempt to make changes to imperfections above this size.

Threshold – Specifies the minimum amount of contrast between pixels there must be before changes are made.

Despeckle Filter

This produces the opposite effect to Add Noise, smoothing and blurring the image, but having little effect on edges.

Median Filter

The Median filter also removes noise from a poor-quality scan. It works by averaging the colour of adjacent pixels in an image.

| To use the Median filter, create a selection, or work on the entire image. Choose Filter > Noise > Median. Specify a Radius value (1–16). OK the dialogue box.

Filter Samples

The following examples of filters provide only a sample of the complete range of filters available in the Filter menu.

Use Command + F (Mac) or Ctrl + F (Windows) to reapply the last-used filter and settings.

It is well worth making a copy of your image to work on before you start experimenting with filters.

Choose Edit > Fade Filter to reduce the effect of a filter on an image.

Original

Artistic

Coloured Pencil   Cut Out

Dry Brush   Film Grain

Brush Strokes

Accented Edges   Angled Strokes

Cross Hatch   Dark Strokes

Distort

Diffuse Glow   Glass

Ocean Ripple   Pinch

Pixelate

Colour Halftone   Crystallise

Facet   Fragment

Render

         Difference
Clouds   Clouds

Lens Flare   Lighting Effects

Original

Sketch

Bas Relief | Chalk and Charcoal

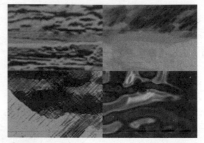

Charcoal | Chrome

Stylise

Diffuse | Emboss

Extrude | Find Edges

Texture

Craquelure | Grain

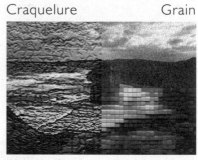

Mosaic Tiles | Patchwork

Other

Custom | High Pass

Maximum | Minimum

Artistic

Fresco | Neon Glow

Paint Daubs | Palette Knife

Web and Multimedia Images

The success of the World Wide Web is in no small part due to its ability to include images in HTML pages. This section looks at some of the considerations for using different image types effectively in formats suited to the environment of the WWW. It also covers techniques for using images in multimedia work.

Balancing file size and image quality is a primary concern when creating images for Web and multimedia use. Generally, the smaller the file size, the quicker the image will load and display on screen. The following techniques examine ways of reducing file size without losing too much image quality.

An image resolution of 72 ppi is usually satisfactory for images intended for screen-based presentations.

Covers

Chapter Fifteen

Save for Web: 2-Up

The Save for Web command offers comprehensive controls for saving images to be used on the World Wide Web. Use the Save for Web command when you want to create an image that is as small as possible – to ensure the fastest possible download times – without sacrificing too much quality.

1 Choose File > Save to save any changes you have made to the image in the current file format. Then choose File > Save for Web (Ctrl/Command+Alt+Shift+S).

Click the 4-Up tab to display versions of the original image, the image using the current optimisation settings, and two other, lower quality variations of the original image, based on the current optimisation settings. (See pages 188–189 for further details.)

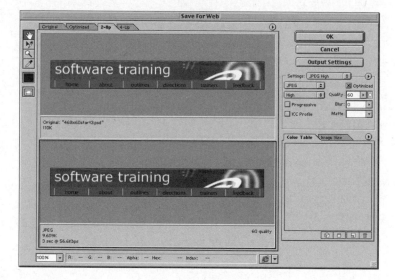

For an image that contains slices, click the Slices Visibility button to view the slices in the Save for Web dialogue box.

2 In the Save for Web dialogue box, click the 2-Up tab to compare the original image and the image with optimisation settings applied. Click the Original tab to view only the original Photoshop image. Click the Optimised tab to view the image with optimisation settings applied. When viewing 2-Up and 4-Up, each optimised pane indicates file format, size, and approximate download time for a specific modem speed in the annotations area.

In ImageReady you can hide/ show the annotations area. Choose View > Hide/Show/ Optimisation Info.

JPEG
2.912K
2 sec @ 28.8Kbps   10 quality

Use the Zoom and Hand tools as you would in the normal image window to zoom in and out and to scroll to different parts of the image.

3 In 2-Up view, make sure the Optimised pane is selected – indicated by a black border. In the Optimise panel, choose an optimisation level from the presets in the Settings pop-up. The Optimised image pane updates so that you can evaluate different options. GIF, JPEG and PNG file formats are discussed later in this chapter.

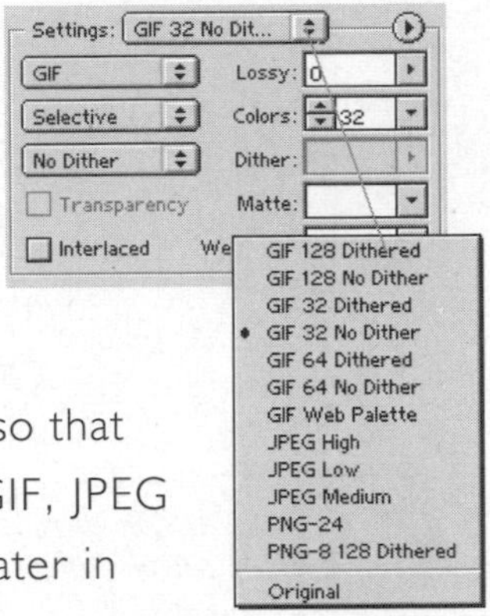

To select a pane click into it. A selected pane is indicated by a black highlight border around the edge.

4 Use the Preview menu to change the download time readout to that expected for a particular modem speed. The readout updates in the annotation area of the optimised preview panes accordingly.

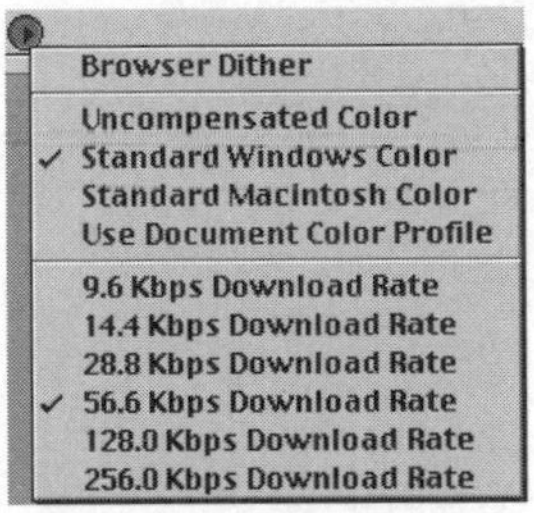

5 Click the OK button when you are satisfied with your settings for the Optimised image. Specify a location and file name using standard Macintosh/ Windows techniques. (See page 190 for further information on saving optimised files.)

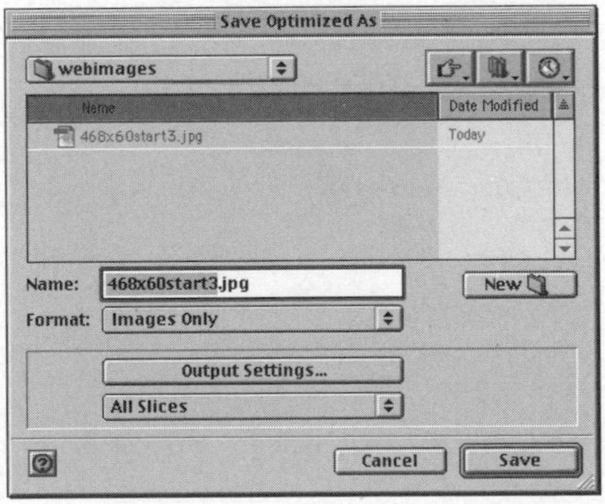

Optimisation: 4-Up View

The Save for Web dialogue box, with the 4-Up tab selected, is particularly useful because it allows you to preview images using a variety of optimisation levels before you decide which level of optimisation you want.

 The arrangement of the 4-Up panes varies according to the size of the Save for Web dialogue box and the dimensions and orientation of the image.

Click the 4-Up tab to view the Original image, the image optimised using the current optimisation settings set in the

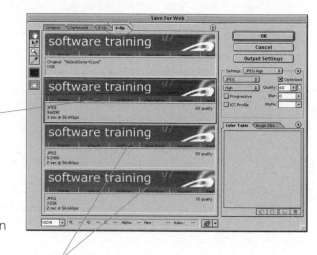

Optimisation panel, and two lower quality variations of the current optimisation settings.

 Use the Zoom and Hand tools to change the magnification and to scroll through images in the preview panes.

2 To change the settings for the Optimised image, click on the Optimised image pane to make sure it is selected. (The typical position for the Optimised image is top right corner of the 4-Up panes.) Choose a new optimisation setting from the presets in the Settings pop-up. The Optimised image pane refreshes to display the results of the new settings.

3 Choose Repopulate views from the Optimisation pop-up to update the remaining panes with lower quality optimisation settings.

The Repopulate command treats the selected pane as the Optimised image, then repopulates the 2 remaining comparison panes with lower quality versions of the optimisation settings.

4 To use one of the lower quality comparison panes as the optimised image, click inside one of the panes to select it. A black highlight border on the pane indicates that it is selected.

For medium to high JPEG compression settings, you can use a small Blur value, e.g. 0.1 to 0.5 to blur pattern artifacts that may appear along sharp edges. Higher values may reduce image detail noticeably.

5 Choose Repopulate Views from the Optimisation panel pop-up. The selected pane becomes the Optimised image and typically appears in the top right corner. Its optimisation settings appear in the Optimisation area. The comparison panes update with lower quality optimisation settings.

To return an optimised version of the image to its original state, select the optimised pane, then choose Original from the bottom of the optimisation Settings pop-up menu.

6 To compare different, unrelated optimisation settings, click on a comparison pane to select it, then choose an optimisation setting from the Settings pop-up. In this case, make sure you do not use the Repopulate Views command.

Preview and Save Optimised Images

You can preview an optimised image in a Web browser before you make a final decision on which optimisation settings to save. This can be a useful check before committing yourself to saving the file.

1 Choose a browser from the Preview pop-up. The browser launches and displays the image from the selected pane. Image details such as file format, dimensions and file size are listed below the image. Below the image details is the HTML code necessary to display the image.

2 To save an optimised image, make sure you select the pane with the settings you want to use. Click OK in the Save for Web dialogue box.

3 Use standard Macintosh/ Windows techniques to navigate to the folder in which you want to save the image. Enter a file name for the image. The file extension for the optimisation settings is automatically appended to the file name. Make sure you don't delete it. The file is saved using the current settings in the Optimise panel.

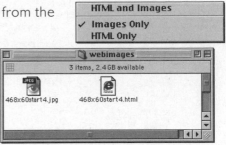

4 Select HTML and Images from the Format pop-up menu, to generate the HTML code necessary to display the image as a separate file. This file is automatically named and saved in the same folder as the optimised image.

The save HTML file option can be most useful when saving images from ImageReady with slices.

5 To specify whether the HTML file uses a table, or Cascading Style Sheets to display an image with slices, click the Output Settings button. Create the settings you require in the Slice Output area of the Output Settings dialogue box.

6 For images that contain slices, use the Slices pop-up menu to choose whether to save all slices in the image, or only the currently selected slice. Each slice is saved as a separate file and named according to the settings in the Output Settings dialogue box.

7 To change the way in which slices are named, in the Output Settings dialogue box choose Slices from the pop-up menu. Use the pop-ups to make changes.

Indexed Colour Mode

Indexed Colour mode is an important factor in the preparation of images for use on the World Wide Web and in multimedia applications. It provides an efficient method for reducing the size of a colour image. When you work on RGB colour images in Photoshop, these are typically 24-bit images, capable of displaying over 16 million colours. Indexed Colour Mode converts images to single channel, 8-bit images, capable of displaying a maximum of 256 colours.

1 To convert an RGB colour image to Indexed Colour mode, choose Image > Mode > Indexed Colour.

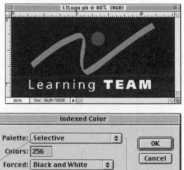

2 Use the Palette pop-up to specify a colour palette which controls and limits the colours that will be used in the image. (See next page.)

3 Choose an option from the Forced pop-up to force the inclusion of certain colours in the colour table.

4 Select Transparency to preserve any transparent areas in the image. Deselect Transparency to fill transparent areas with the Matte colour. White is used if there is no Matte colour selected. Matte is only available if there are areas of transparency. (See page 197 for more information.)

5 Set dithering options. (See page 195).

Colour Palettes

A colour palette controls the 256 possible colours that exist in an Indexed Colour image. Photoshop/ImageReady uses three methods for creating colour tables in images: dynamic, fixed and custom.

Dynamic – Perceptual, Selective and Adaptive colour palettes are created dynamically. Each time you optimise the image, the palette created is based on the colours occurring in the image. Different images will generate different palettes.

When working with GIF compression settings you can also choose colour palettes from the Palette pop-up in the Optimise area of the Save for Web dialogue box in Photoshop and the Optimise Palette in ImageReady.

Fixed – the Web, Mac OS, Windows, Black & White and Greyscale colour palettes are fixed. There is a limited, or fixed range of colours. If your optimisation settings specify less than 256 colours, this reduced range of colours is drawn from the fixed colour table.

```
Exact
System (Mac OS)
System (Windows)
Web
Uniform

Perceptual
✓ Selective
Adaptive

Custom...

Previous
```

Custom – Custom palettes use colours created or modified by the user. Existing GIF and PNG-8 files also have custom palettes.

Exact

If the image you are converting already has fewer than 256 colours, Exact is the default. The actual number of colours is indicated in the Colours entry box. You cannot dither an Exact palette.

System Palettes

This is the standard, 8-bit system palette of either the Macintosh or Windows system.

Web

This is a palette reduced to 216 colours. Use this palette to achieve consistency across different platforms and when you want to use more than one image on the same Web page. Images which are based on different colour palettes can look artificial when seen side by side.

Uniform

This palette is based on a uniform sampling of colours from the colour spectrum.

Adaptive

This palette is built around the colours that actually occur in an image. For individual images, it gives better results than Web, as the colour table is created by sampling colours from the most frequently occurring areas of the colour spectrum in the image.

Custom

This option takes you into the Colour Table dialogue box and allows you to create your own custom colour table.

Previous

Previous is only available after you have converted an image using either Adaptive or Custom methods. It uses exactly the same palette as created by the previous conversion.

Perceptual

The perceptual option creates a colour palette biased towards colours to which the human eye is most sensitive.

Selective

This is similar to Perceptual, but biased towards broad areas of colour in the image and also the preservation of Web colours. Selective is the default.

You can specify an exact number of colours for an Indexed Colour image if you don't want the maximum 256 steps. Enter a value in the Colours field.

Palette:	Selective
Colors:	256
Forced:	Black and White
☒ Transparency

Dithering

Dithering is a technique that simulates colours that are not actually in the colour palette. On computer monitors that support only 256 colours, dithering takes place to simulate a greater range of colours in an image than the monitor is actually capable of displaying. For Web images this is referred to as browser dither. Dithering juxtaposes pixels of different colours to create the illusion of additional colours.

Dithering is not recommended for JPEG images.

To minimise the occurrence of browser dither, create the image using only Web-safe colours.

Images with areas of solid colour may compress best with Dither set to None. Images with gradients usually need dithering to prevent obvious banding.

Choose a dithering method for an image when you optimise it. This is referred to as application dither – the dither is built into the image.

1 Choose an option from the Dither pop-up. For Diffusion, set a Dither Amount. Higher values result in more dithering which creates the appearance of a greater number of colours in the image. Higher values can also increase the file size, depending on the image.

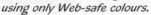

2 Select Preserve Exact Colours to protect colours in the colour table from being dithered.

None
No dithering is applied to the image.

Pattern
This creates a square dither pattern, similar to halftones, to simulate colours not available in the colour table.

Diffusion
The results of Diffusion are usually less noticeable than Pattern as the dithering is spread across a range of pixels.

Noise
Applies a random dither pattern. This option can be used for images with slices.

Saving Indexed Colour Images as GIFs

When you have converted an image to Indexed Colour mode, you can then use the standard Save as command to save the image in GIF format.

This technique works best for flat coloured images such as logos. For photographic type images with subtle colour transitions, JPEG is a better method of preparing images for the World Wide Web.

1 To save the image in GIF format, choose File > Save As. Specify CompuServe GIF from the Format pop-up menu. Specify a location for saving the file and enter a name. Make sure you use the '.gif' extension. OK the dialogue box.

Name: 468x60start3.gif

Format: CompuServe GIF

2 Click the Interlaced option in the GIF Options dialogue box if you want a low-resolution image to download first, followed by progressively more image information as it becomes available from the Web server.

GIF Options

Row Order
- ◉ Normal
- ◯ Interlaced

OK

Cancel

Avoid using GIF format if your image contains a gradient. Use JPEG format instead (see page 197).

JPEG Format for Web Images

For a general introduction to JPEG format, see page 47.

JPEG is a compression format, widely used for preparing images for the World Wide Web. Use JPEG when you are working with photographic-type images, and when preserving colour detail and quality in the image are more important than download time considerations. JPEG does not allow transparency, and file sizes may be larger than for images exported in GIF format, depending on the compression level you choose.

Save images with gradients in JPEG format, as JPEG format produces smaller file sizes than GIFs with an Adaptive palette.

1 To save an image in JPEG format, choose File > Save As. Specify a location, enter a name, then choose JPEG from the Formats pop-up. OK the dialogue box.

2 Choose a colour from the Matte pop-up to simulate background transparency in the image. You need to know the background colour of the Web page, to match the matte colour to it. (Use the Save A Copy command to be able to access the Matte pop-up.)

JPEG is most suited to compressing continuous-tone images (images in which the distinction between immediately neighbouring pixels is slight). JPEG is not the best format for saving flat colour images.

3 Use the Quality pop-up to specify the amount of compression, or drag the slider. 'Maximum' gives best quality, retaining most of the detail in the image, but least compression. 'Low' gives lowest image quality, but maximum compression.

4 For Format Options, choose Baseline Optimised to optimise the colour quality of the image. Select Progressive and enter a number for Scans to download the image in a series of passes which add detail progressively until the image is completely displayed. Click OK to export the file.

PNG File Format

PNG is a relatively new file format for saving images for use on the Web. There are 2 PNG file format options: PNG-8 and PNG-24.

PNG-8

PNG-8 file format uses 8-bit colour which allows a maximum of 256 colours in an image. It is most effective at compressing areas of solid, flat colour, typically found in line art, logos and illustrations with type.

PNG-8 is a lossless compression formula – no colour information is lost during compression. Depending on the image, PNG-8 compression can produce files 10–30% smaller than the same image compressed using GIF format.

PNG-8 file format can support background transparency and background matting. Background matting enables you to blend the edges of an image into the background colour you set as the background colour of your Web page.

PNG-24

PNG-24 supports 24-bit colour which allows millions of colours in the image. Like JPEG, this is a good format when you want to preserve subtle transitions in tone and colour in a photographic type image.

PNG-24 uses a lossless compression formula – no colour information is discarded during compression. As a result, PNG-24 file sizes are typically larger than if you save the image using JPEG file format.

PNG-24 supports background transparency and background matting. PNG-24 also supports multilevel transparency which allows greater control over the way in which an image blends into the background colour of a Web page.

Working with ImageReady

With the rapid, commercial development of the World Wide Web since mid 1990's onward, there has been a growing need for a distinct set of controls and features that allow the user to create eye-catching, optimised images with small file sizes for rapid download times on modems. Creating images for the Web brings a different range of possibilities and technical requirements and constraints when compared with creating images destined to be printed on paper.

ImageReady is designed specifically to meet these rapidly emerging needs. It has dedicated optimization controls, you can create animated GIF files, Slices, Rollovers and background images.

Covers

Chapter Sixteen

Photoshop and ImageReady

ImageReady and Photoshop exist as separate application environments, yet work side by side with one another. Much of the tool set and many of the palettes and working techniques are identical in both environments. ImageReady is specifically optimised for creating images for the Web and multimedia, whereas Photoshop provides a powerful feature set for creating images for print, but at the same time provides controls for the creation of images destined for the screen.

You can work on an image in Photoshop, then continue to make further adjustments to the same image in ImageReady, or vice versa. Use the Jump to button or command to move images seamlessly from one environment to the other so that you can work in the environment that gives you the most control for whatever task you are attempting.

The majority of the ImageReady palettes have the same range of functionality as their counterparts in Photoshop.

The Animation, Slice, ImageMap and Rollover palettes are available in ImageReady only.

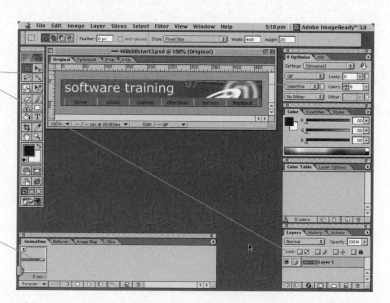

Jumping Between Applications

For an image you've begun to prepare in Photoshop, choose File > Jump to then Image Ready from the sub menu. Or click the Jump To button.

Although you can work on an image in two different applications, there is only one image file. Changes you make in one environment can be used to update the image in the other environment. To avoid confusion - always ensure that changes you make in one environment are saved and that you update these changes to the image in the other environment when prompted.

Individual or multiple changes you make in one application environment are represented in the History palette of the other application as a single entry called 'Update from File'.

Depending on which application environment is active, clicking on an image window of the other application also has the effect of the Jump to command.

Follow the same procedures outlined here when you create a new image in ImageReady and move it into Photoshop.

2 Image Ready then launches and the image appears in the ImageReady application window. You can now make further changes to the image in ImageReady. (The image remains open in the Photoshop application environment.)

3 To move the image currently active in ImageReady back into the Photoshop working environment again, click the Jump to button, or choose File > Jump to, then select Adobe Photoshop from the sub menu.

4 When you are moving an image between applications, both files in each application have the same file name. Think of this as having an active copy, the one you are working on in the currently active application environment, with the other file as a live backup. It is best, as far as possible, to keep these two files synchronised. The best way to achieve this is to choose Edit > Preferences > General. Select the Auto-Update files option.

The ImageReady Toolbox & Image Window

The ImageReady Toolbox is largely the same as the Photoshop Toolbox. This page indicates the tools found in ImageReady which are not found in Photoshop, illustrating how to create Tear-off tool groups.

To create a Tear-off tool palette, position your cursor on a tool group (indicated by the small triangle). Press and hold the mouse button, then move it onto the Tear-off bar at the bottom of the palette, then release the mouse button.

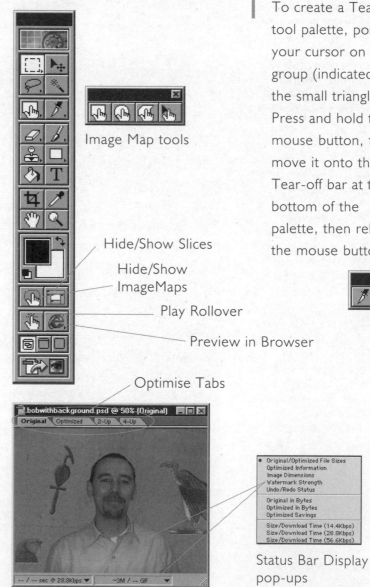

Image Map tools

Hide/Show Slices

Hide/Show ImageMaps

Play Rollover

Preview in Browser

Optimise Tabs

Status Bar Display pop-ups

Creating and Saving Images

Although creating and saving images in ImageReady is very similar to the same routines in Photoshop, there are some differences to be aware of.

In ImageReady's New Document dialogue box there is no colour mode pop-up. Images in ImageReady are always in RGB mode.

1 To create a new file in ImageReady, choose File > New. Enter values in pixels for Width and Height, or change the existing values by clicking on the increment arrows. There is no need to give the file a name at this stage.

In the ImageReady New Document dialogue box you do not set a resolution. The resolution of images in ImageReady is always 72 ppi.

2 Choose an option for the Contents of First Layer. Select White to fill the default layer with White. Choose Background to fill the layer with the current Background colour. Choose Transparent to create a transparent layer.

3 To save a file, in the first instance, choose File > Save as. In the Save Original dialogue box, specify a location in which you want to save the file. Enter a name. Notice that the .PSD file extension is automatically added to the file name. Make sure you retain the file extension. Click the Save button.

You work in Photoshop file format (.PSD) as you build and edit an image. Optimise the image when you have finished working on it and want to prepare it for the WWW.

4 Continue to work on the file in Photoshop format and use the Save command (Ctrl/Command+S) regularly to save changes you make.

5 Use the Status bar pop-ups to choose readouts that help you make decisions about the image on which you are working.

169K / 11.05K GIF ▼	173,308 bytes ▼

● Original/Optimized File Sizes
　Optimized Information
　Image Dimensions
　Watermark Strength
　Undo/Redo Status

　Original in Bytes
　Optimized in Bytes
　Optimized Savings

　Size/Download Time (14.4Kbps)
　Size/Download Time (28.8Kbps)
　Size/Download Time (56.6Kbps)

Make sure you are working in the Original tab to edit and change the image.

6 When the image is finished and you want to save an optimised version for use on the World Wide Web or in a multimedia application, use the Save Optimised As command. (See pages 212–213 for information on saving optimised files.)

Layer Effects in ImageReady

ImageReady's Layer Effects are largely similar to those in Photoshop, but there are some important differences to be aware of.

1 To create a layer effect, click on the layer you want to modify to select it.

2 In addition to options in the Layers > Layer Styles sub-menu, you can use the Layer Effects pop-up in the bottom of the Layers palette to choose an effect.

When you create a new image in ImageReady, the first, default layer is layer 1. ImageReady does not have a default Background layer as its first layer like Photoshop. When you move a Photoshop image into ImageReady, the Background layer is converted into Layer 0 and treated as any other layer.

3 Options for specifying aspects of the effect are located in the Effects palette which displays appropriate controls according to which effect is selected in the Layers palette pop-up. (See pages 125–126 for information on Bevel and Emboss layer effects in Photoshop.)

4 Click the collapse triangle to hide the names of any layer effects applied to a layer. This is a useful space saving option in complex illustrations using multiple layer effects. Click the collapse/expand triangle to show any layer effects applied to the layer.

5 Drag a layer effect name into the Wastebasket in the Layers palette to delete it. Alternatively, select a layer effect name, then click the Wastebasket icon. Click Delete in the Warning prompt.

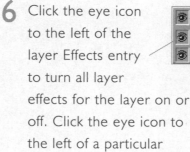

6 Click the eye icon to the left of the layer Effects entry to turn all layer effects for the layer on or off. Click the eye icon to the left of a particular effect to hide/show that specific effect only.

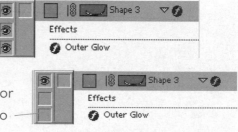

7 The Bevel and Emboss and Gradient Pattern and Outer Glow palettes have additional options which may not be showing. Choose Show/Hide Options from the pop-up menu, or click the expand button in the palette tab.

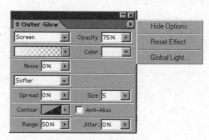

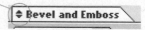

Handling Type in ImageReady

Type is entered and edited directly in the image window, as it is in Photoshop.

Choose the Vertical Type tool to create vertical type.

1 To enter type, choose the Type tool, position your cursor in the image window, then click to place the text insertion point.

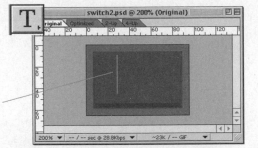

When you create type in ImageReady you do not access the Type Tool dialogue box as you do in Photoshop.

2 Enter type using the keyboard. The type automatically creates a new type layer in the Layers palette. The new layer is positioned above the previously active layer. Type appears formatted with the current settings in the Type palettes.

You should consider using slightly larger type when working with images for the Web than you would for printed images.

3 To make changes to the formatting of type, select the Type tool, then drag across the text in the image window. You can highlight type in this way, even if the type layer is not active.

4 To change type settings, with the Type tool selected, choose options from the Options bar.

When choosing an anti-aliasing level for type, make sure you are viewing the image at actual size to get the best feel for how the type will appear when viewed by the end user.

5 Click the Palettes button in the Options bar to display the Character and Paragraph palettes.

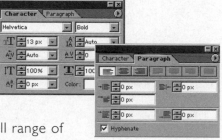

These palettes offer the full range of controls available in Photoshop and ImageReady. (See pages 140–142 for information on using the Character and Paragraph palettes.)

Pixels are the only unit of measurement for type.

6 When a type layer is active, when you choose any tool other than the type tool, the type highlights with a blue line running across the base of the type and a small square indicating the current alignment setting for the type.

7 To reposition type, make sure the type layer is active, select the Move tool, then drag the type.

The Shape Tools

Shapes you create with the Shape tools are bitmaps that appear on the active layer if you create a filled shape, or vector objects that automatically generate a new layer if you create a new shape layer.

Use the Rectangle, Rounded Rectangle, Ellipse and Line tools to create either a new shape layer, or a filled shape. The techniques for using each tool are the same.

1 To draw a rectangle or oval or line, choose the appropriate tool. Select either the New Shape Layer button, or the Filled Shape button.

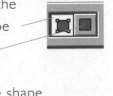

To move or transform a shape layer, click on the shape layer icon in the Layers palette.

This automatically selects the Move tool and a transform bounding box appears around the shape. (See page 129 for information on transforming layers.)

2 If you selected New Shape Layer button, the shape automatically creates a new layer. Use the Options bar to create settings for the shape layer. You can use the Style pop-up to apply a pre-defined Layer Style to a shape layer.

3 If you selected the Filled Shape button, the shape appears as a rasterised shape (a shape that consists of pixels) on the active layer. Select Fixed Size to create a shape to precise dimensions. Choose anti-aliased (Ellipse and Rounded Rectangle) to help the object blend into its background by creating a slightly soft edge.

There is no Direct Selection tool in ImageReady. If you want to edit the vector path of a shape layer, jump to Adobe Photoshop.

To create a square or a circle, hold down Shift and drag with the Shape tool. Start to drag with a Shape tool, then hold down Alt, to draw a shape from the centre out.

4 Position your cursor in the image window, then press and drag to create the shape. Release the mouse when the object is the required size. The object fills with the current foreground colour.

The ImageReady Optimise Palette

The basic principles for optimising images in ImageReady are the same as in Photoshop Save for Web dialogue box (see pages 186–189). The main difference is that the Original, Optimised, 2-Up and 4-Up tabs are part of the ImageReady window and therefore always available. The optimisation settings and controls are located in the Optimise palette.

The purpose of optimising an image is to create an acceptable balance between image quality and download times.

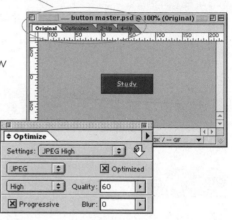

1 Choose Window > Show Optimise if the Optimise palette is not already showing.

2 Use the Settings pop-up menu to choose one of the pre-defined optimisation settings. The optimised image pane updates according to the settings you choose.

When you choose new optimisation settings for the optimised image pane, the remaining panes in 4-Up view do not update automatically. Choose Repopulate from the Optimise palette pop-up menu to repopulate the other panes with lower quality versions of those in the optimised pane.

3 Use the 2-Up and 4-Up tabs to compare the visual quality of different optimisation settings, along with file format, file size and download time readouts. To hide or show annotations in the 2-Up/4-Up views, choose View > Hide/Show Optimisation Info.

4 In 4-Up view, select an optimised version of the image – a black highlight border appears around the selected pane. Choose Repopulate views from the pop-up menu in the Optimise palette. The selected version now

becomes the Optimised version and ImageReady automatically generates two smaller, lower quality versions of the optimised image in the two remaining panes.

5 When you begin working with Optimisation settings, use the pre-defined settings in the Settings pop-up as the basis for optimising images.

6 To restore an optimised version of the image to the original version, first select the optimised version, then choose Original from the Settings pop-up menu.

7 If optimising an image to a specific file size is more important than the resultant image quality, choose Optimise to File Size from the Optimise palette pop-up menu. Enter the required file size. Select the Auto Select GIF/JPEG options to allow ImageReady to choose the most effective compression format. Choose Current settings to use the current format as the basis for reducing the file size.

Saving an Optimised Image

When you have decided on optimisation settings that give you the correct balance between image quality and file size, you can then save an optimised version of the file.

1   Choose File > Save to save any changes to the image in the original Photoshop file format.

2   If you are working with the Optimised tab selected, check that the current optimisation settings in the Optimise palette are the ones you want. Alternatively, choose Optimisation information from the Status bar pop-ups. Then choose File > Save Optimised As.

3   If you are working in 2-Up view, make sure the Optimised pane is selected. A selected pane is indicated by a black highlight border. Choose File > Save Optimised As.

4   If you are working with the 4-Up tab, make sure you select the pane with the settings you want to use for optimising the image. Then choose File > Save Optimised As.

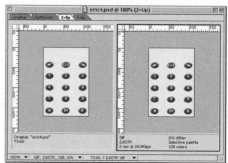

5 In the Save Optimised dialogue box, specify a location and a name for the file. The appropriate file format extension (e.g. .gif) is appended automatically. Make sure you retain the file extension. Leave the Save Images option selected.

If you are working on an optimised image, in 2-Up or 4-Up view, when you choose File > Save Optimised, the settings you save are those of the selected image pane.

6 Select the Save HTML File option to save an additional HTML file that includes the image name, its dimensions in pixels and any other code necessary to display the image on a Web page. The HTML file is saved as a separate file with a .html extension in the same folder as the image file. This option is most useful when you are saving images with slices (see Chapter 18.)

7 Select the Save Selected Slices only when you have selected specific slices in the image prior to choosing the Save Optimised As command. ImageReady creates a complete HTML table capable of displaying the selected slices.

GIF Optimisation Settings

The GIF file format usually provides the most efficient and flexible optimisation controls for images which have areas of flat colour, with sharp edges and type, such as you often find in logos and buttons.

1 To optimise an image using GIF file format, select the image pane for which you want to create the settings. To create a setting for a slice, use the Slice Select tool to select a slice.

You cannot use the Lossy option with the Interlaced option, or with a Noise or Pattern dither.

2 Choose one of the preset GIF settings from the Settings pop-up menu.

3 Or, to create custom GIF settings, choose GIF from the format pop-up, then specify settings using the options in the palette.

4 Drag the Lossy slider, or enter a value to reduce file size by discarding colour information. Values of 5–10 can often be applied without noticeably degrading the image quality.

5 Choose a colour palette (see pages 193–194) and a dither method (see page 195).

6 Use the Colours pop-up menu to specify the maximum number of colours in the Colour palette. Images can consist of fewer colours than the number specified.

Animations

Animations are built from a series of GIF images which, when displayed in quick succession, create the illusion of movement. You create and control animations using the Animation and Layers palettes in ImageReady.

Animations can bring impact, movement and variety to a Web page, but they can also become distracting if not used carefully. Use animations when they bring dynamism to a page and contribute to the message and content. Don't use animations for their own sake.

Covers

Chapter Seventeen

Creating a Simple Animation

Animations can range from the very simple to the very complex. Try to keep your animations simple at the outset. Remember that animation effects, if used indiscriminately on Web pages, can be distracting and as a result lose their intended impact.

When you open or create an image in ImageReady, the image becomes the first frame in the Animation palette by default, even if you do not intend to create an animation.

1 Create an image in Photoshop, or directly in ImageReady as in this example. Use Layers as the basis for the animation. The layers you create form the basic building blocks for the animation. Put elements you want to animate on separate layers.

To avoid confusion as you create an animation, make sure that you have created and finished editing all the objects and layers you want to use, before you start to build the animation.

2 Hide any layers containing elements you do not want to appear at the start of the animation.

3 Choose Window > Show Animation to show the Animation palette if it is not already showing. Choose New Frame from the palette's pop-up menu, or click the New Frame button. This creates frame 2, which is a duplicate of the preceding frame.

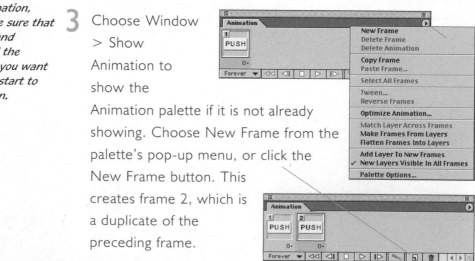

Animations are saved in GIF file format. JPEG and PNG formats cannot be used for animations.

When working in ImageReady, it is best to create and edit the animation in Original view. Options for editing animations are more limited in Optimised view.

Any changes you make on a layer that affect actual pixel values, for example, painting, changing colour or tone, or using transform commands, will affect all frames in the animation in which the layer is present.

4 Make a change to a layer. Changes you make to the layers, such as layer visibility, position, opacity or layer effects, form the animation when the frames are viewed in quick succession. In this example the 'P' is moved next to the 'U'.

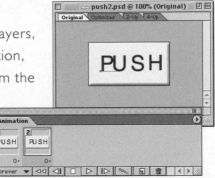

5 Repeat Steps 3–4 as necessary. In this example, both the 'P' and 'U' are moved to the 'S'. Then, for the final frame, the 'P', 'U' and 'S' are moved up to the 'H'.

6 Save the animation in Photoshop format as you build and make changes. This means you can return to the original file, if necessary to make further adjustments. (See pages 220–221 for information on saving an optimised version of the animation for use on the Web.)

Playing and Managing Frames

As you build an animation you will need to preview it and to control aspects such as looping and frame rate.

To select multiple, consecutive frames, click on the first frame, hold down Shift, then click on the last frame in the range you want to select. To select nonconsecutive frames, click on a frame to select it, hold down Ctrl/Command, then click on other frames to add them to the previously selected frame.

1 To play an animation, click the Play button. The animation plays in the image window and each frame in the Animation palette highlights in sequence as the animation plays.

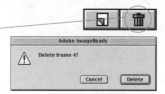

2 Click the Stop button to stop the animation at the current frame.

3 To select a frame, click on the frame in the Animation palette. The frame highlights and becomes the current frame. The current frame is displayed in the image window. It is the frame that can currently be edited.

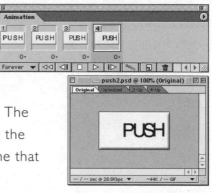

When you select multiple frames, you can distinguish the current frame by the black highlight border around the frame.

4 To delete a frame, first click on it to select it. Then click the Wastebasket button at the bottom of the palette. Click the Delete button in the warning dialogue box. Alternatively, drag the frame into the Wastebasket, or choose Delete Frame from the pop-up menu in the palette.

5   To change the position of a frame, select the frame you
    want to move, then drag it to a new location. Release the
    mouse when you see a
    thick black bar at the
    position to which you want
    to move the frame.

*Preview
animations in
a browser to
get an
accurate idea
of the delay you specify.*

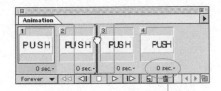

6   To set the frame delay rate (the speed at which
    frames advance), first select a frame, or multiple
    frames. Use the Frame Delay pop-up located
    below each frame. Either
    choose a value from the
    preset list, or choose other,
    then specify a delay in the Set
    Frame Delay dialogue box.

7   To specify looping options, use the Loop pop-up in the
    bottom left corner of the Animation palette.
    Forever plays the animation in a continuous
    loop. Choose Other to specify a set number of
    times you want the
    animation to play. Enter a
    value in the Play ... times
    field.

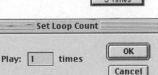

Optimising and Saving Animations

When you have created the frames for your animation and you are satisfied with the effect, you can optimise and then save the animation.

1 To optimise an animation, click the Optimise tab in the ImageReady window. In the Optimise palette, choose the optimisation settings you want to use from the Settings pop-up.

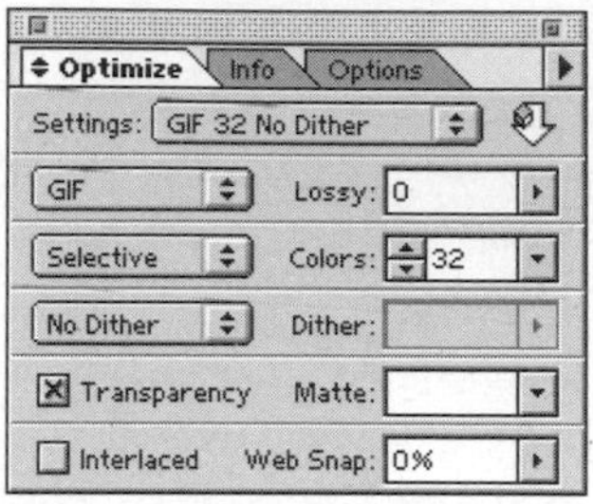

2 To preview the results of the optimisation settings, choose File > Preview in, then choose from the list of available browsers. The browser launches and the animation plays in the browser window. File format information and HTML code are displayed below the animation for information purposes. Close the browser.

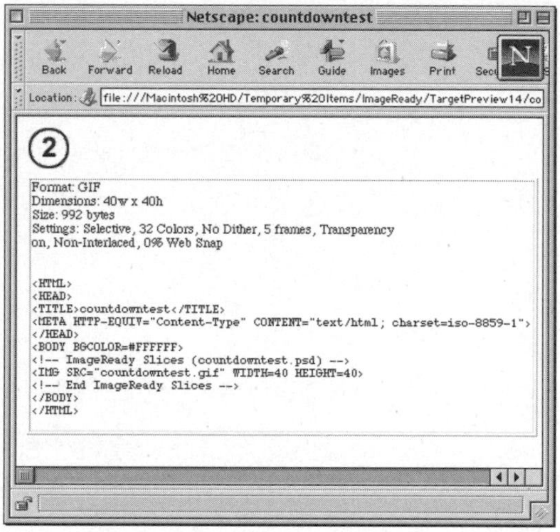

3 Test other optimisation settings and preview until you are satisfied with the results.

4 To save the animation, choose File > Save Optimised As. Use standard Macintosh/ Windows techniques to specify a location and a name for the file. Make sure you retain the .GIF file extension which should appear automatically.

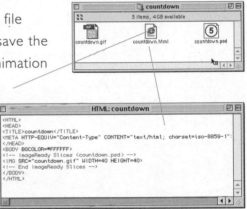

5 Select the Save HTML file option if you want to save the HTML code for the animation file. The HTML file is saved in the same folder and with the same name as the animation, but with an HTML file extension.

6 Make sure you leave the Save Images option selected. Click the Save button.

Tweening

In ImageReady, the Tween command allows you to create smoother animations quickly and easily, by automatically creating additional frames between existing frames in the animation. These additional, in-between frames create smoother movement in the animation.

The term 'tweening' is derived from a traditional animation term 'in betweening' where additional frames were created between key frames to create smooth animation effects.

1 To tween a frame, first click the New Frame button to create a duplicate of the first frame.

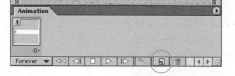

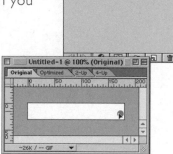

2 Make a change, for example reposition an object, to the layer on which you are working.

Use tweening to dramatically reduce the amount of time needed to create smooth animations.

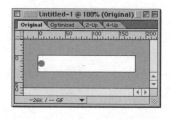

Tweened animation frames do not require a new layer for each new frame. The tweening effect takes place on an individual layer.

3 Click the Tween button in the animations palette, or choose Tween from the palette pop-up menu.

4 For Layers, select the Selected Layers option to vary only the currently selected layer in the selected frame, otherwise leave the option set to All Layers.

5 Choose Parameter options to specify which elements you want to

You can tween the last and first frames in an animation. This is useful to create a smooth transition from the end of an animation back to the beginning, when the animation is designed to loop a number of times.

tween. In this example it is important to choose Position, as it is the position of the layers in the animation that vary. Select Opacity if opacity settings vary between frames. Select Effects if Layer Effects vary between frames.

Parameters:	☐ Position
	☒ Opacity
	☐ Effects

6 Use the Tween with: pop-up to choose the frame with which you want to tween the currently selected frame.

	Selection
Tween with:	✓ Next Frame
	Last Frame

7 Enter a value in the Frames to Add field to specify the number of in-between frames. The more in-between frames you add, the smoother the animation, but the result is a larger file size.

8 OK the dialogue box. The in-between frames are added as new frames. Subsequent frames are renumbered accordingly.

Copying and Pasting Frames

You can copy a frame or multiple frames and then paste the copied frame(s) into a new location in the current animation, or into a completely different animation.

| To copy a frame, first select the frame. A black highlight indicates the frame is selected.

2 Choose Copy Frame from the Animation palette pop-up menu.

3 Select a frame in which you want to paste the copied frame. Choose Paste Frame from the Animation pop-up menu.

4 Choose an option for Paste Method, then click OK.

5 Hold down Shift, then choose Paste Frame to paste the copied frame after the currently selected destination frame.

Slicing and Image Maps

Slicing allows you to create a single, complete image in Photoshop or ImageReady, then sub-divide it into specific areas – the slices. ImageReady automatically generates the HTML code for a table that will hold the sliced image, or the code that will display the image using Cascading Style Sheets.

Using slices you can optimise parts of an image differently for different purposes; slices can become buttons and assigned links; and you can also create rollover states for slices. The functionality of slices varies slightly between Photoshop and ImageReady.

Use Image Maps to define areas of an image as clickable hypertext links in a Web page.

Covers

Chapter Eighteen

Slices from Guides and the Slice Tool

Create the image in Photoshop if you need to work to a visible grid. Image Ready does not support grids.

Slices are rectangular areas of an image that become the contents of a single cell in an HTML table, or that can be coded using Cascading Style Sheets. An image in ImageReady initially consists of a single slice by default, comprising the complete image. When you create a new slice, the remainder of the image is automatically divided into further slices.

You can create slices based on ruler guides or selections, or you can create a slice using the Slice tool. This section looks at techniques for creating slices from guides and using the Slice tool.

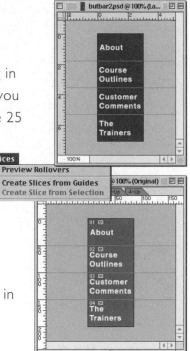

When you use the Create Slices from Guides command, ImageReady deletes previously created slices.

Slices from Guides

1   Create or open an image. Drag in ruler guides to indicate where you want to create slices. (See page 25 for information on creating ruler guides.) Click the Jump To button if you are not already working in ImageReady.

Any image in ImageReady initially consists of one slice which is comprised of the entire image. When you create a new slice, ImageReady automatically divides the rest of the image into further, additional slices that will fit into a HTML table.

2   Choose Slices > Create Slices from Guides. The slices appear in the image. Each slice is numbered. Slices created from guides are User-slices. (See page 229 for information on User- and Auto-slices.) A colour adjustment, visible when slices are showing is applied to slices to indicate User- and Auto-slices. (See page 229 for further information.)

When you use the Create Slices form Guides command, all existing slices are deleted.

Slices you create using the Create Slices from Guides command and using the Slice tool are created as User-slices.

3 Choose the Slice Select tool (A), then click on a slice to select it. A coloured bounding box appears around the slice, defining the area of the slice.

4 The selected slice also appears in the Slice palette. Choose

Window > Show Slice if the palette is not already showing.

The Slice Tool

1 To create a slice using the Slice tool, click on the tool to select it. Position your cursor on the image, then drag to define the area of the slice. The slice you define is a User-slice.

Slices are rectangular areas of an image that become the contents of individual cells in an HTML table. When loaded in a browser, the image appears to be a single, composite image. In HTML terms, it is split into discreet, separate areas.

2 When you release the mouse, ImageReady automatically generates additional slices to enable the image to fit into an HTML table. The additional slices are Auto-slices.

3 Hold down Shift as you drag with the Slice tool to create a square slice. Hold down Alt as you drag to create the slice from the centre out.

As soon as you select the Slice tool, existing slices display automatically.

4 Choose View > Snap to > Slices if you want the Slice tool to snap to other slices or guides. The snap takes effect when your cursor comes within 4 pixels of a slice or guide.

Creating Slices from Selections

You can also create slices from selections.

When you click the Hide Slices button (Q), the colour adjustments applied to slices disappears.

1 Create a selection. Choose Slice > Create Slice from Selection. The selection becomes a User-slice. (See page 229 for information on User and Auto-slices.) The User-

You cannot create slices from selections in Photoshop.

slice is numbered and the remainder of the image is divided into further slices as necessary to fit the complete image into an HTML table, or for coding as Cascading Style Sheets. The User-slice is selected and a highlight bounding box appears around it. A colour adjustment is applied to the remainder of the image. This colour adjustment is helpful in distinguishing between User- and Auto-slices.

If you create a slice from a feathered selection, the slice includes the feathered area.

2 Continue creating slices as necessary. As you create additional slices, slice numbers are updated. Slices are numbered from left to right and top to bottom.

If you use a non-rectangular selection to create a slice, the slice itself covers a rectangle that encompasses the complete selection.

User- and Auto-slices

You can promote an Auto-slice to a User-slice. In Photoshop select the Promote to User-slice option in the Options bar. In ImageReady choose Slices > Promote to User-slice.

A slice can have one of two statuses: User or Auto. There are more possibilities for modifying User-slices. Any slices you create (using guides, selections or the Slice tool) are User-slices. Slices created automatically by ImageReady to enable the remainder of the image to fit into an HTML table are Auto-slices. An image in ImageReady automatically consists of one Auto-slice compromising the full image.

You can change or 'promote' an Auto-slice into a User-slice. User-slices can be assigned different optimisation settings. Auto-slices in an image are initially linked and therefore share the same optimisation settings. The link symbol which appears next to Auto-slices indicates that they share the same optimisation settings.

The colour adjustment applied to slices dims the brightness and contrast of unselected slices. This is for display purposes only. The colour adjustment does not affect the final colour of images.

There are two types of slices: Image or No Image. Image slices contain image information – pixels. No Image slices can contain a solid colour, or HTML text. An Image slice is

identified by the image icon when slices are visible.

Starting in the top left corner, slices are numbered from left to right and top to bottom. As you add, delete and rearrange slices, slice numbers are updated automatically.

User-slices have blue slice annotation symbols; Auto-slices have grey slice annotation symbols.

User-slices are indicated by a solid boundary line; Auto-slices by a dotted line.

Different colour adjustments on User- and Auto-slices and the slice information icons help you distinguish the two statuses. The colour adjustment on User-slices is half the strength of the colour adjustment used to distinguish Auto-slices.

Working with Slices

Use the following techniques to hide and show slices and to select and deselect slices.

1 To hide slices and slice information such as slice number and slice type icons, click the Hide/Show Slice button (Q) in the Toolbox. To show slices, click the button again (Q).

2 To select a slice, select the Slice Select tool (A). Click on a slice. A coloured bounding box with eight selection handles appears around the slice indicating it is selected. The colour adjustment, which defines the area of the slices, is switched off for the selected slice.

3 To select multiple slices, select a slice, hold down Shift, then click inside another slice to add it to the selection.

4 When you select a slice, it appears in the Slice palette. Choose Window > Show Slice to show the Slice palette if it is not already showing. The slice number and file format of the slice are indicated below the slice thumbnail. (See page 232 for information on assigning URLs to slices so that they can function as buttons on a Web page.)

Photoshop and ImageReady can generate slices as a HTML table, or as Cascading Style Sheets. In the Save Optimised As dialogue box (see page 190), click the Output settings button to specify which method is used.

To delete a slice, first select it, then press the Backspace or Delete key. Auto-slices are automatically created to cover the complete image.

In Photoshop, to hide/show slice numbers, use the Show Slice Numbers option in the Options Bar.

You cannot move or resize User-slices in the Photoshop Save for Web dialogue box.

To delete all User-slices, in Photoshop choose View > Clear Slices; in ImageReady choose Slices > Delete All.

5 Choose File > Preview in, then select a Browser from the sub-menu to preview the image in the browser window. The automatically generated HTML code for the sliced image is also displayed in the browser window.

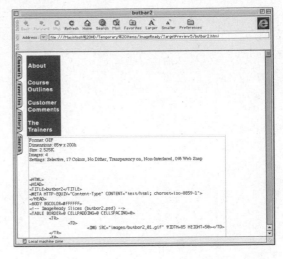

6 Use the Optimise palette to create optimisation settings for the image. (See Chapter 16 for details). You can create different optimisation settings for individual slices if required.

7 Choose Save Optimised As to save an optimised version of the image. (See page 212 for information on saving optimised images).

8 To move a slice, select the Slice Select tool, position your cursor within the slice you want to move, then drag the slice.

9 To resize a slice, select the Slice Select tool. Select a slice, then drag a side or corner resize handle.

Assigning URLs to Slices and Image Maps

You can make a slice or image map act as a clickable button that will link to another Web page by assigning a URL to the slice or image map area.

1 Select the Slice tool to select a slice. Select the Image Map select tool to select an image map area. Click on a slice or image map to select it. Make sure the Slice or Image Map palette is showing. The selected slice appears in the Slices palette. Information for a selected Image Map area appears in the Image Map palette.

When you assign a URL to an Auto-slice it becomes a User-slice.

With either the Slice or Slice Selection tool selected, hold down Command/Ctrl to toggle temporarily to the other tool.

2 Slices and Image Map areas are automatically named. An underscore and a slice/image map number are added in the name field.

3 Enter a URL in the URL entry field. You should include the http:// specifier at the beginning of the URL for absolute paths. You can also specify relative paths. You can choose any previously created URL from the URL pop-up menu.

4 If you are preparing images for a Web site that uses frames, specify a target frame – where the HTML file you link to will appear – using the Target entry field. Enter the name of the target frame exactly as defined in the frameset file.

Image Maps

The Image Map tools and palette allow you to create areas in an image that become clickable hyperlinks when the image is used in a HTML file. Unlike slicing and image, where individual slices become separate files, creating an image map keeps the image as a single file, with areas of the image defined as links. As well as rectangular areas, image maps enable you to create circular and irregular areas to act as links.

With the Rectangular or Elliptical Image Map tool selected, hold down Shift to create a square or circle.

1 To create an image map, select one of the Image Map tools. Press and drag diagonally to create rectangular or oval image map areas. For the Polygon Image Map tool, position your cursor on the image, click, move the cursor to a new position (do not click and drag), then click again. Repeat this process to create the shape you require. Click back at the start point to close the shape. You can also double-click to close the shape.

2 To show existing image map areas in an image, select the Image Map Select tool, or choose View > Show > Image Maps. You can also click the Image Map Visibility button in the Toolbox to show/hide image map areas in the image window.

3 Use the Image Map Select tool to select areas of an image map. Click in an image map area to select it.

4 To reposition an image map area, position the Image Map Select tool in the area, then press and drag the area in the image window.

5 To resize a selected image map area, position the Select cursor on one of the resize handles on the area's border, then press and drag.

6 You can also control the size and position

of a selected image map area in the Dimensions section of the Image Map palette.

7 To delete an image map area, select it, then press the Backspace or Delete key.

Index